EXCAVATIONS AT NANTACK VILLAGE
POINT OF PINES, ARIZONA

DAVID A. BRETERNITZ

NUMBER 1

ANTHROPOLOGICAL PAPERS

OF THE

UNIVERSITY OF ARIZONA

TUCSON

1959

DEDICATED TO
ARNOLD M. WITHERS

CONTRIBUTIONS TO POINT OF PINES ARCHAEOLOGY

NUMBER 13

[Complete list on page 77]

PREFACE

FIELD WORK at Nantack Village was done during the 1954 and 1955 seasons of the University of Arizona Archaeological Field School at Point of Pines on the San Carlos Indian Reservation, Arizona. The field school is jointly sponsored by the Arizona State Museum and the Department of Anthropology at the University of Arizona. Work was done under permit from the San Carlos Apache Tribal Council and the United States Department of the Interior.

Excavations in 1954 were supervised by Daniel J. Scheans; in 1955 I was the supervisor. Work was done by students of the University of Arizona Archaeological Field School and in 1955 by an Apache Indian, Ole Harvey. The students were: 1954, Galen Baker, William Beeson, David Breternitz, Frank Holtzkamper, Herbert Lewis, Daniel Scheans, Tacoma Sloan; 1955, Takey Dabbagh, Frank Eddy, Leonard Fonaroff, John Garrett, Oskar Grunow, Lee Hubbard, Ernest Leavitt, A. J. Lindsay, Jr., Robert Loud, Ralph Zepp.

Nantack Village was mapped by Dr. Emil W. Haury, Roberts Wallace, Daniel J. Scheans and me. Dr. E. B. Danson, Christy G. Turner II, Daniel J. Scheans and I took the excavation photographs. L. F. H. Lowe made the photographic plates of specimens.

Faunal material was identified by Milton A. Wetherill; James E. Officer examined the shell. Stone implements were identified by Leo Heindl, United States Geological Survey, and R. T. O'Haire, Arizona Bureau of Mines. William J. Beeson, James C. Gifford, Alan P. Olson and Dick Shutler, Jr. were consulted on certain pottery type classifications.

Wilma Kaemlein supervised the field cataloging of specimens and assisted in making available the material on its arrival in Tucson.

Arthur H. Rohn, Jr. permitted me to use data obtained from a microscopic study of Encinas Red-on-brown pottery.

The excavations at Nantack Village were the subject of a thesis submitted as partial fulfillment of the requirements for a Master's degree at the University of Arizona (Breternitz 1956). Drs. Emil W. Haury, Edward B. Danson and Bertram S. Kraus served as members of the thesis committee. Additions, revisions, and corrections of this thesis were done under the guidance of Dr. Haury and Dr. Raymond H. Thompson.

The cooperation and encouragement of a great many colleagues is reflected in this work, especially that of James C. Gifford, Alan P. Olson and Barton A. Wright. Dr. Olson provided the author with many specific details of the Reserve and Tularosa Phases at Point of Pines. Mr. Wright drafted six of the figures.

DAVID A. BRETERNITZ
Museum of Northern Arizona
July 1, 1959

CONTENTS

1. **INTRODUCTION** 1
   - Nantack Village and the Nantack Phase 1
   - Location and Environment 1
   - Excavation Procedure 4
2. **THE NANTACK PHASE OCCUPATION** 5
   - Architecture 5
     - Houses with Lateral Entry 5
       - Pithouse 1 5
       - Pithouse 3 7
       - Pithouse 4 7
       - Pithouse 5 10
       - Pithouse 6 10
       - Pithouse 8 13
       - Pithouse 9 15
     - House with no Lateral Entry 15
       - Pithouse 2 15
     - Unclassified House 16
       - Pithouse 7 16
     - Ceremonial Structures 16
       - Great Kiva 16
       - Pithouse 10 19
     - Pits outside Houses 19
     - Discussion 22
       - Relative Dating 24
   - Pottery 24
     - Plainware 24
     - Redware 25
     - Textured Pottery 25
       - New Type: Pine Flat Neck Corrugated 25
     - Painted and Intrusive Pottery 29
       - New Type: Nantack Red-on-brown 29
       - Hohokam Intrusives 30
       - Mimbres Intrusives 30
       - Other Intrusives 30
     - Whole Vessels 32
       - Miniature Vessels 32
     - Miscellaneous Pottery Objects 33

Discussion	34
Trash Mound	34
Plainware	34
Redware	34
Textured Pottery	35
Painted and Intrusive Pottery	35
Miscellaneous Pottery Objects	35
Stone Artifacts	38
Ground Stone	38
Metates	39
Grinding Slabs	39
Manos and Handstones	40
Pestles	41
Stone Bowls	41
Stone Dish	42
Pitted Tuff Discoids	42
Stone Ring	42
Palettes	42
Effigies	42
Problematical Stone	43
Polishing Stones	43
Abrading Stones	43
Grooved Abrading Stone	43
Shaped Stones	43
Hammerstones	44
Grooved Mauls	44
Grooved Tuff Cobble	44
Three-quarter Grooved Axes	44
Ornaments	44
Minerals	44
Curios	45
Discussion	45
Flaked Stone	46
Projectile Points	46
Knives	48
Drills	49
Scrapers	49
Flake Gravers	49
Blades-Saws	49
Stone Disc	49
Choppers	50
Discussion	50
Bone, Antler, and Shell Artifacts	50
Bone	51
Awls	51
Miscellaneous	51
Antler	51
Shell	51
Discussion	52
Synopsis of the Nantack Phase	52
Trait List	52

CONTENTS

3. THE POST-NANTACK PHASE OCCUPATION 55
    Architecture 55
        Ruin B 55
        Ruin C 56
            Room 1 56
            Room 2 56
            Room 3 57
        Discussion 59
    Pottery 60
        Plainware 62
        Redware 62
        Textured Pottery 62
        Painted and Intrusive Pottery 62
        Whole Vessels 63
        Miscellaneous Pottery Objects 63
        Discussion 64
    Artifacts 64
        Ground Stone 64
            Metates 65
            Grinding Slabs 65
            Manos 65
            Handstones 65
            Polishing Stones 65
            Abrading Stones 65
            Grooved Abrading Stone 65
            Hammerstones 65
            Grooved Maul 65
            Minerals and Curios 65
        Flaked Stone 66
            Projectile Points 66
            Knives 66
            Scrapers 66
            Blades-Saws 66
        Bone 66
        Discussion 66
    Summary 66

4. BURIALS 67
        Burial 1 67
        Burial 2 67
        Burial 3 67
        Burial 4 68
        Summary 68

5. CONCLUSIONS 69
    Dating 69
        The Chronological "Gap" 70
    Community Pattern 72
    Summary 72
    REFERENCES 73

ILLUSTRATIONS

1.	Map of Nantack Village	2
2.	Plan and sections of Pithouse 1	6
3.	Pithouse 1	7
4.	Pithouse 3	7
5.	Plan and sections of Pithouse 3	8
6.	Plan and sections of Pithouse 4 and Ruin B	9
7.	Pithouse 5	10
8.	Plan and sections of Pithouse 5	11
9.	Plan and sections of Pithouse 6	12
10.	Pithouse 6	13
11.	Pithouse 8	13
12.	Plan and sections of Pithouse 8	14
13.	Plan and section of Pithouse 2	15
14.	Plan and sections of Pithouse 7 and Ruin C, Room 2	16
15.	The Great Kiva	17
16.	Plan and sections of Great Kiva	18
17.	Plan and sections of Pithouse 10	20
18.	Pithouse 10	21
19.	Vessel shapes of Alma Plain, Point of Pines Variety	25
20.	Redware vessel shapes	25
21.	Jars of Three Circle Neck Corrugated, Point of Pines Variety	26
22.	Vessel shapes of Pine Flat Neck Corrugated	27
23.	Jars of Pine Flat Neck Corrugated	27
24.	Sherds of Pine Flat Neck Corrugated	28
25.	Red-on-brown sherds	29
26.	Jar of Mangas Black-on-white	30
27.	Jar of Wingate Black-on-red	31
28.	Miniature vessels	32
29.	Sherd discs	33
30.	Fragment of unidentified clay object and incised sherd	34
31.	Metates	39
32.	Grinding slab and pestle	40
33.	Manos and handstones	41
34.	Stone bowls, stone dish, and pitted tuff discoid	41
35.	Painted stone bowl	42
36.	Palettes, effigies, and problematical stone	43
37.	Grooved tuff cobble and three-quarter grooved axes	44
38.	Projectile points, drill, and flake gravers	47
39.	Knives	48
40.	Scrapers and drill	49
41.	Blades-saws and chipped disc	49
42.	Bone, antler, and shell artifacts	51
43.	Ruin B, Room 3, wall detail	56
44.	Ruin C, Rooms 1 and 3	57
45.	Plan and sections of Ruin C, Rooms 1 and 3	58
46.	Vessel shapes of plainware	62
47.	Brownware ceramic tubes	63
48.	Phase sequence	71

TABLES

1. Architectural Characteristics of Semi-subterranean Structures 23
2. Plain, Red, and Textured Sherds from Pithouses, Great Kiva, and Burials . . . 36
3. Painted and Intrusive Sherds from Pithouses, Great Kiva, and Burials . . . 37
4. Sherds from Surface Structures 61
5. Pottery Cross-Dating for Mogollon 4 Phases 70

1

INTRODUCTION

NANTACK VILLAGE AND THE NANTACK PHASE

NANTACK VILLAGE was selected for study because its prehistoric occupation included a period of time, from A.D. 900–1000, that was not well understood in the Point of Pines chronology. Numerous tests and the excavation of 11 semi-subterranean units, including one Great Kiva, now make possible the definition of the Nantack Phase. This term has been chosen to designate a particular cultural manifestation in the Point of Pines area which differs from those preceding and following it (Fig. 48). This use of the cultural phase concept is consistent with accepted archaeological usage in the Southwest.

In addition to the excavations undertaken to obtain information about the Nantack Phase, six surface rooms, occupied after A.D. 1000, were also dug at Nantack Village. They were excavated in order to obtain stratigraphic information concerning the wider range of cultural material found at the site and also to aid in determining the end date for the Nantack Phase.

LOCATION AND ENVIRONMENT

Nantack Village, which is designated Arizona W: 10: 111 in the Arizona State Museum Archaeological Survey (Wasley 1957), is located one mile south of the University of Arizona Archaeological Field School, Point of Pines, Arizona (Fig. 1). Detailed descriptions of the environment and geography of the region are to be found elsewhere (Gifford 1957; Wendorf 1950; Wheat, 1952, 1954).

The site is on a finger-like extension of the Nantack Ridge which trends in a general southwest to northeast direction and rises 15 to 20 meters above the minor drainages which parallel the ridge on either side. The ridge is about 250 meters long and 25 to 50 meters wide on the crest. The maximum elevation is 1860.5 meters (6040 feet) above sea level.

Western Yellow Pine *(Pinus ponderosa)*, Alligator bark juniper *(Juniperus deppeana)*, and Live oak *(Quercus sp.)* frequently grow within the pithouse depressions.

Low rock mounds and boulder alignments are the surface indications of structures. Additional surface rooms were found which were covered by a mat of pine needles and forest humus obscuring indications of a structure. At least 10 surface rooms on the north end of the ridge were noted but not excavated.

Sheet trash, which results from the broadcasting of debris over an area and is a characteristic of sites of the Mogollon Culture, extended over the top and sides of the ridge to an average depth of 15 to 25 cm. Rodent activity was extensive at the site, especially in the two trash mounds.

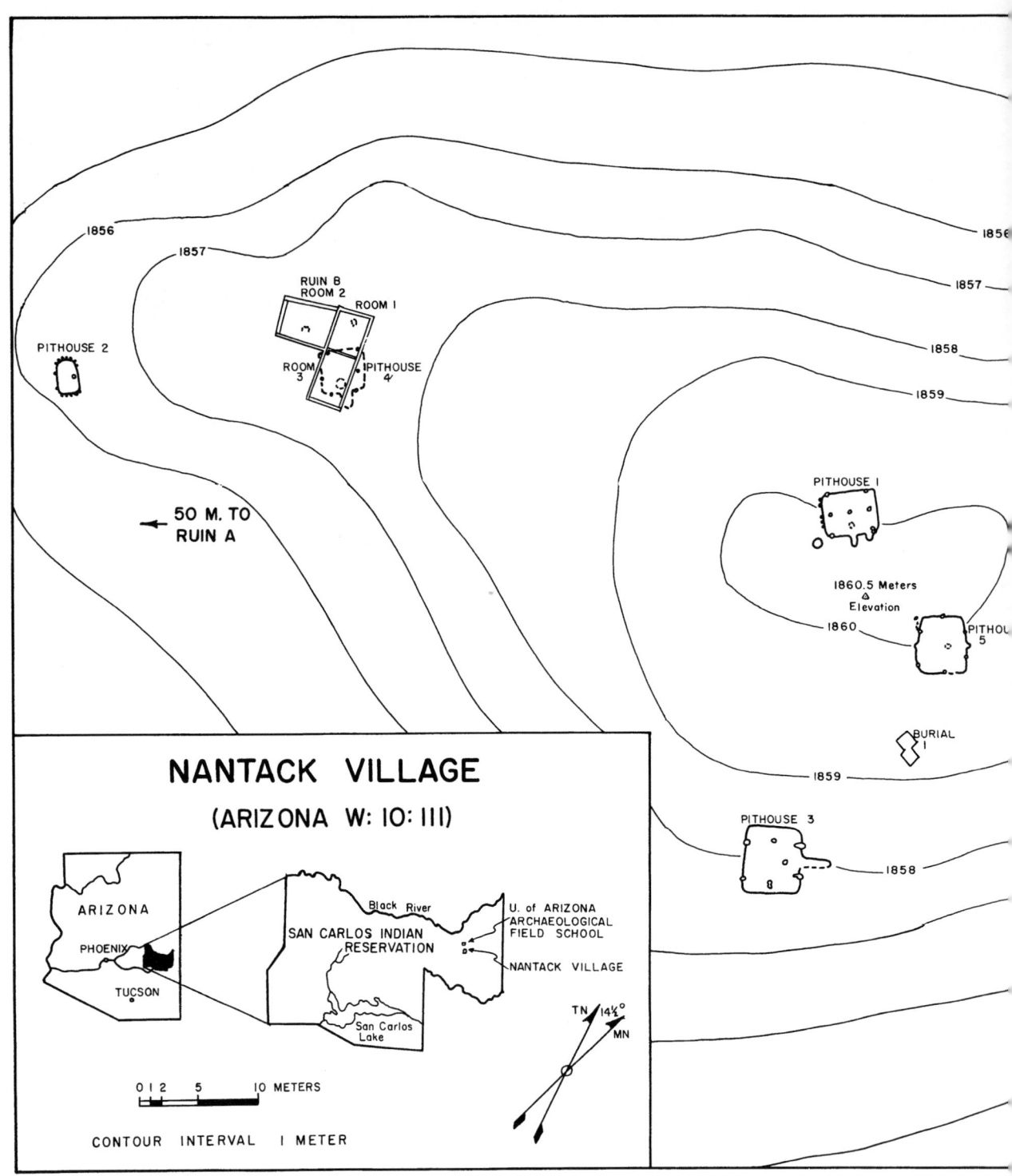

Fig 1. Map of Nantack Village.

INTRODUCTION

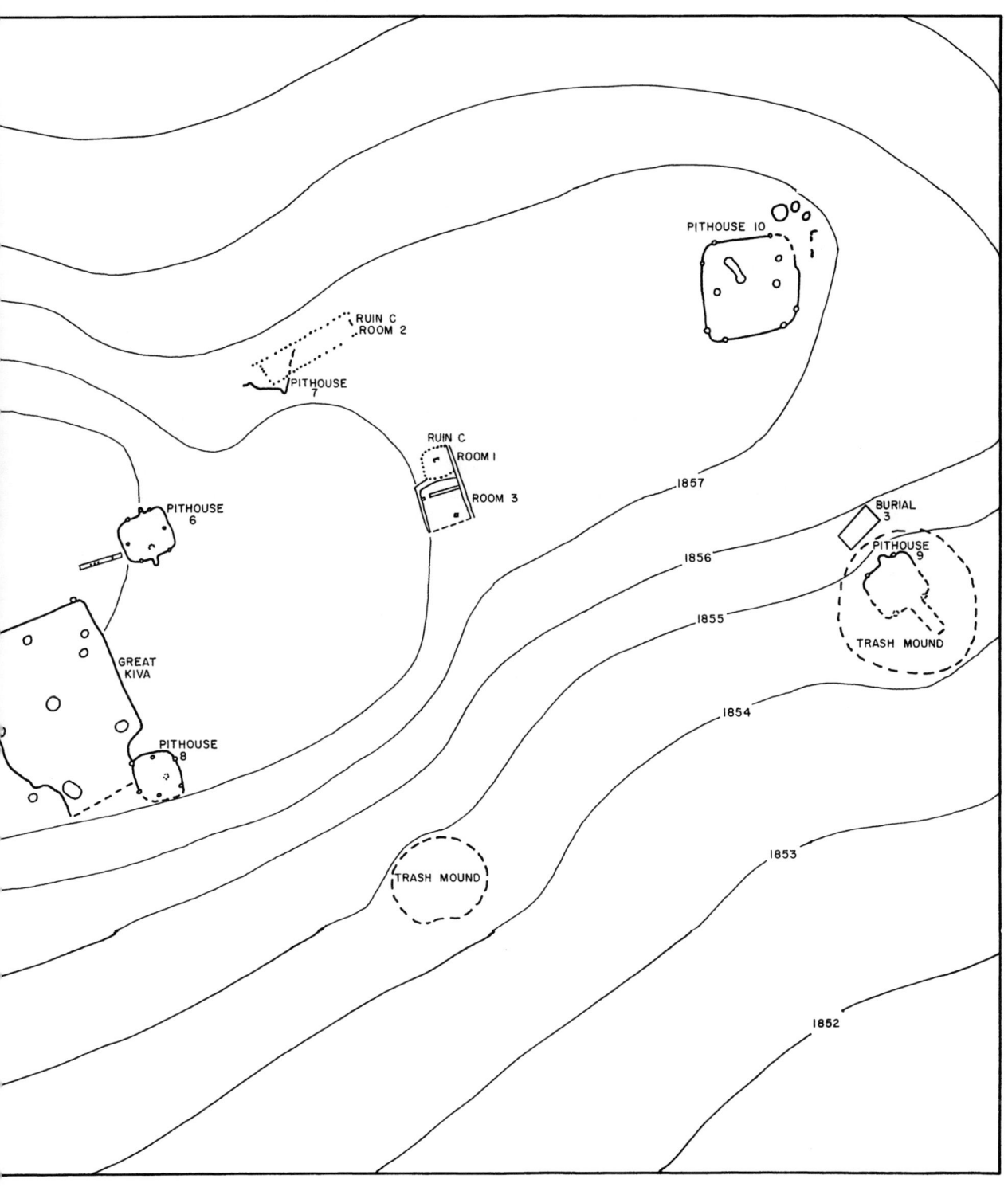

Native soil is found beneath the sheet trash and shallow forest humus. This is highly compacted conglomerate composed of yellow clay containing pebbles of leucite tuff. Where there are no man-made disturbances the organic soil-humus grades into the yellow native clay in a mixed-native layer which is brownish in color. The cleavage between trash and clay is distinct in both color and texture.

The following contemporary animals were observed at Nantack Village during excavations: bear *(Ursus sp.)*, deer *(Odocoileus hemionus)*, rabbit *(Lepus sp.)*, and Merriam's turkey *(Meleagris gallapavo merriami)*.

Represented in the archaeological collections are:

Flora—A round, flat, charred seed; species unidentifiable.

Fauna—White tail deer *(Odocoileus virginianus)*, Mule deer *(Odocoileus hemionus)*, jackrabbit *(Lepus californicus)*, prairie dog *(Cynomys arizonensis)*, dog *(Canis sp.)*, and turkey *(Meleagris gallapavo)*.

EXCAVATION PROCEDURE

The system of pithouse and surface room nomenclature was initiated during the 1954 field season and continued the following year.

Nantack Village was surveyed with a plane table and alidade (Fig. 1). A line was established roughly following the crest of the ridge. All excavation units were plotted from datum stations along this line.

Series of test pits in lines were used as an exploratory technique. These were arbitrary and placed where it was hoped they would divulge maximum information. Pithouses 2 and 3 were found as a result of these test pits.

A soil sampling tube (Wheat 1954: 15) was also used to find pithouses, after the average depth of the sheet trash was determined from the test pits. Probings with the soil sampling tube, which went deeper than 35 cm. before penetrating native yellow clay, indicated the presence of a structure. Pithouses 1, 4, 5, 6, 7, 9, and 10 were thus found.

Pithouses were excavated by digging a one by two meter test pit to the floor and the floor was followed to a wall. The wall area was trenched to within 10 to 15 cm. of the floor. The resultant core was taken out in 25 cm. levels to within 10 to 15 cm. of the floor. The remaining floor fill was excavated after the area adjacent to the pithouse was stripped. Portions of the area around Pithouses 1, 3, 5, 6, 8, and 10 were cleared to the native yellow clay, in search of outlying postholes, pits, or other features. When the remaining floor fill was removed, the cultural material in contact with the floor was left in place until photographed.

Excavation of the Great Kiva was begun in 1954 and completed the following year. Test pits were dug to roughly establish the limits of the structure and the back (west) wall was trenched. Roughly two-thirds of the central core were taken out as a single level and designated kiva fill. Termination of the 1954 field season necessitated protective backfilling. In 1955 this backdirt was removed and that portion of the Great Kiva excavated the previous season was cleared to the floor. Because the fill left above the floor in the western two-thirds of the Great Kiva did not exceed 15 cm. in depth it was excavated as one level and designated floor fill. The eastern one-third was dug as one level due to the slope of the ridge and the shallowness of the trash. This eastern one-third of the fill was combined with the kiva fill material of the 1954 season. Material from the large postholes was kept separate for use as an artificial stratigraphic control. It was hoped that the posthole fill material, primarily potsherds, would augment the few specimens which were found on the floor of the Great Kiva.

Surface rooms were excavated in 25 cm. levels whenever possible. The shallowness of surface units accounts in part for the difficulty in dating these structures.

Artifacts not catalogued were measured, sketched and described on five by eight inch cards, following a system of notation in use at the University of Arizona Archaeological Field School.

2

THE NANTACK PHASE OCCUPATION

ARCHITECTURE

AT NANTACK VILLAGE nine semi-subterranean structures were completely excavated and two were partially dug. Surface depressions and testing with the soil sampling tube indicated the presence of several additional subsurface units.

The 11 semi-subterranean units are assigned to the following types on the basis of shape, position of entrance, and presumed use:

   Houses with Lateral Entry (7) Pithouses 1, 3, 4, 5, 6, 8, 9
   Houses with No Lateral Entry (1) Pithouse 2
   Unclassified House (1) Pithouse 7
   Ceremonial Structures (2?) Great Kiva, Pithouse 10 (?)

Tabulation of artifacts found on the floor includes broken and partial specimens. Magnetic north is indicated on the plans.

Houses With Lateral Entry

Pithouse 1

Illustrations: Figs. 2, 3.

Dimensions: North-south, 4.40 m.; east-west, 4.05 m. Depth from present surface, 0.90 m.

Walls: Bottom of walls formed by pit excavated into native clay. Tuff boulders resting on native clay along south wall are probably for basal support of jacal upper wall. Shallow wall niche in northeast corner.

Entrance: Oriented towards southeast; stepped. Length, 1.30 m.; width, 0.35 m.

Floor: Shallowly concave. Remnants of floor plaster on native clay around hearth area; extent is estimated in Figure 2 since it was not accurately recorded. Depression beneath hearth.

Hearth: Located between foot of entrance and center of pithouse; rock-lined except for short northeast arc; 0.15 m. deep, filled with ash.

Pits: Storage pit, slightly bell-shaped, outside southeast corner of pithouse. (Discussed further in section on Pits Outside House.) Catch basin(?) located at foot of the entrance, 0.18 m. deep.

Postholes: Seven main postholes; two pairs of postholes recessed into front and back walls, one is double; two postholes in line with recessed pairs and single central posthole. All main postholes found from floor level; 17 secondary postholes not found until patches of floor plaster were removed.

Material culture on floor: 14 manos and handstones, 7 metates, 11 hammerstones, 2 clay balls, 1 projectile point, 1 stone quadruped effigy, 1 perforated sherd, 1 shaped stone-mano blank, 1 polishing pebble, 1 bottom of Reserve Red jar, 1 neck of Pine Flat Neck Corrugated jar; 2 stone bowls from bottom of northeast (double) posthole; 1 maul from floor of storage pit; half of San Francisco Red jar from wall niche.

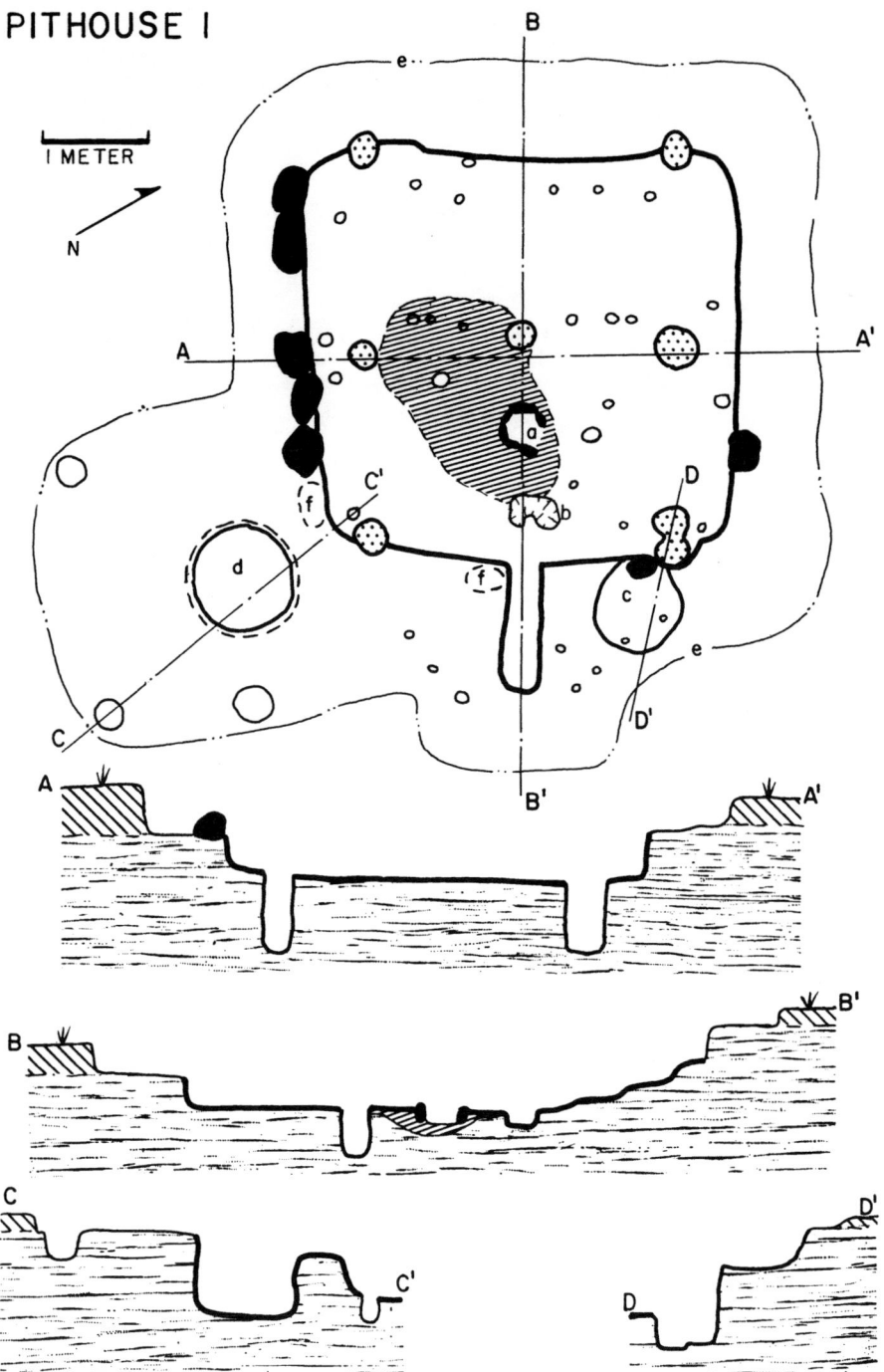

Fig. 2. Plan and sections of Pithouse 1. Horizontal streak, native clay; wide hatching, trash; black, rock; narrow hatching, floor plaster; stipple, main postholes; a, hearth; b, catch basin; c, wall niche; d, storage pit; e, limit of excavation; f, rock removed during excavation. Unlettered features indicated by circles are secondary postholes.

Fig. 3. Pithouse 1. Arrow indicates magnetic north.

Remarks: Before the entryway was cleaned to native clay a possible three-step entry was found. At the top of the first two risers was a rock and the top step was the native clay shown in cross-section B-B¹ of Figure 2. This is evidence of remodeling, as is the occurrence of secondary postholes beneath the plastered floor and the depression beneath the hearth.

Pithouse 3

Illustrations: Figs. 4, 5.

Dimensions: North-south, 4.38 m.; east-west 4.80 m. Depth from present surface, 1.25 m.

Walls: Bottom portion of walls formed by pit excavated into native clay. Plaster along north and east walls; some plaster burned. Shallow coping at bottom of west and south walls appears to be base for wall plaster, but could be the result of excavating the floor to a deeper level after the pithouse was constructed.

Entrance: Oriented towards northeast; ramp with terminal step. Length, 2.50 m.; width, 0.60(?) m.

Floor: Plaster spotty over level floor of packed native clay.

Hearth: Possible hearth in front of entryway; clay depression with no ash.

Postholes: Pair of recessed postholes in front and back walls; postholes in front wall both double, and one divided by plaster on trashy fill. Two other main postholes; one double.

Material culture on floor: 2 manos, 1 metate, 1 grinding slab, 1 Reserve Red bowl, 1 Alma Plain jar, 1 Three Circle Neck Corrugated jar; 2 stone bowls and 1 stone ring from northeast posthole fill.

Remarks: Pithouse 3 was built partly into trash. Post-1000 pottery types are from the surface unit upslope from the pithouse, to the north. The lower edge of this surface unit is indicated by the rock slabs in Figure 5. Pithouse 3 burned but none of the six charcoal specimens was datable. Many pieces of burned roofing clay were found in the fill 20 to 30 cm. above the floor.

Pithouse 4

Illustrations: Fig. 6.

Dimensions: North-south, 4.15 m.; east-west, 3.60 m. Depth from present surface, average, 0.80 m.

Walls: Bottom of walls formed by pit excavated into native clay.

Entrance: Oriented towards northeast; ramp with terminal step. Length, 1.70 m.; width, 0.80–1.00 m.(?).

Floor: Spotty indications of plaster on irregular native clay floor.

Fig. 4. Pithouse 3. Plaster flush with pithouse wall may be seen in the large double posthole next to the meter bar.

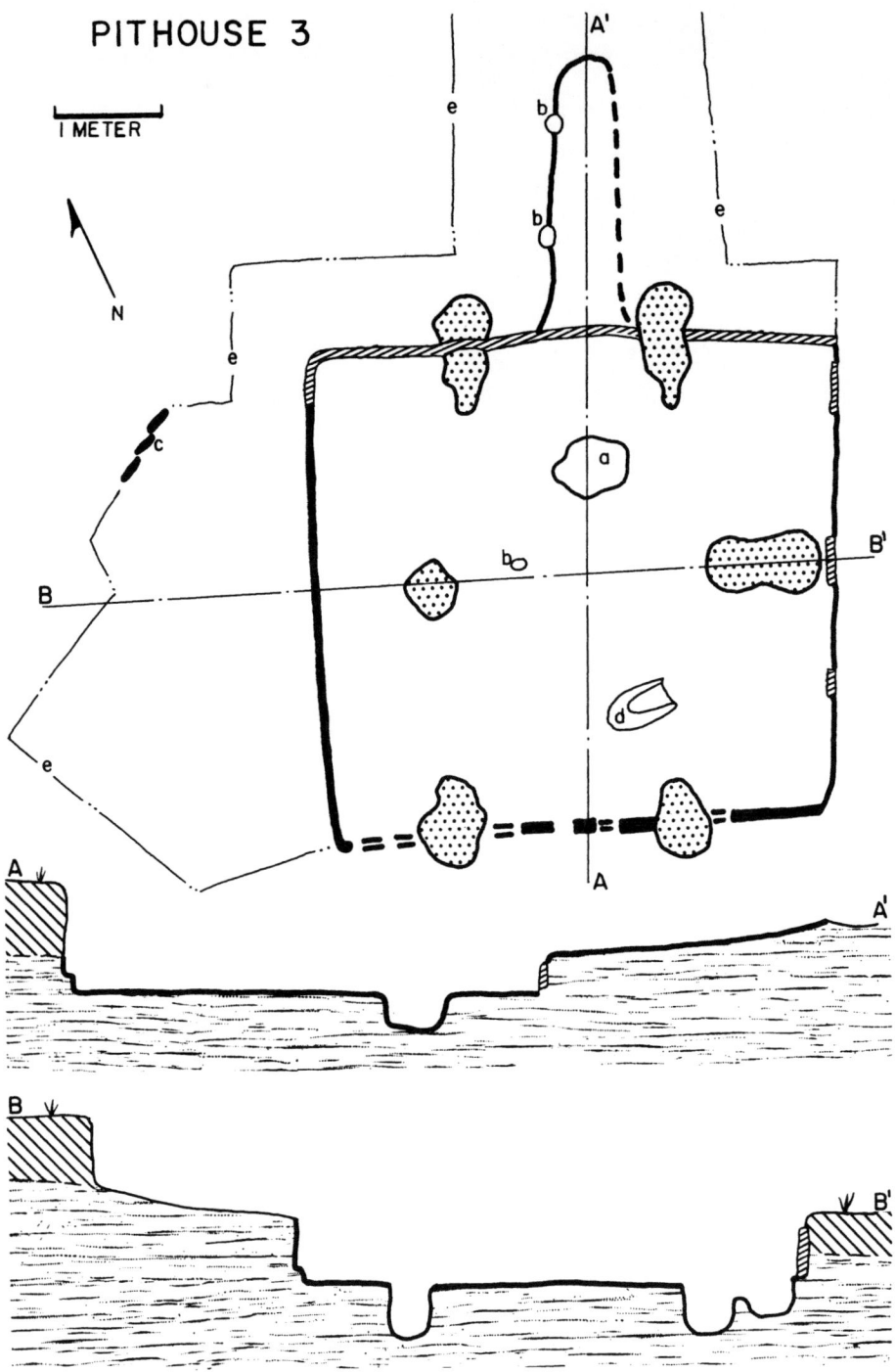

Fig. 5. Plan and sections of Pithouse 3. Horizontal streak, native clay; wide hatching, wall plaster; stipple, main postholes; *a*, hearth; *b*, secondary postholes; *c*, slabs; *d*, metate; *e*, limit of excavation.

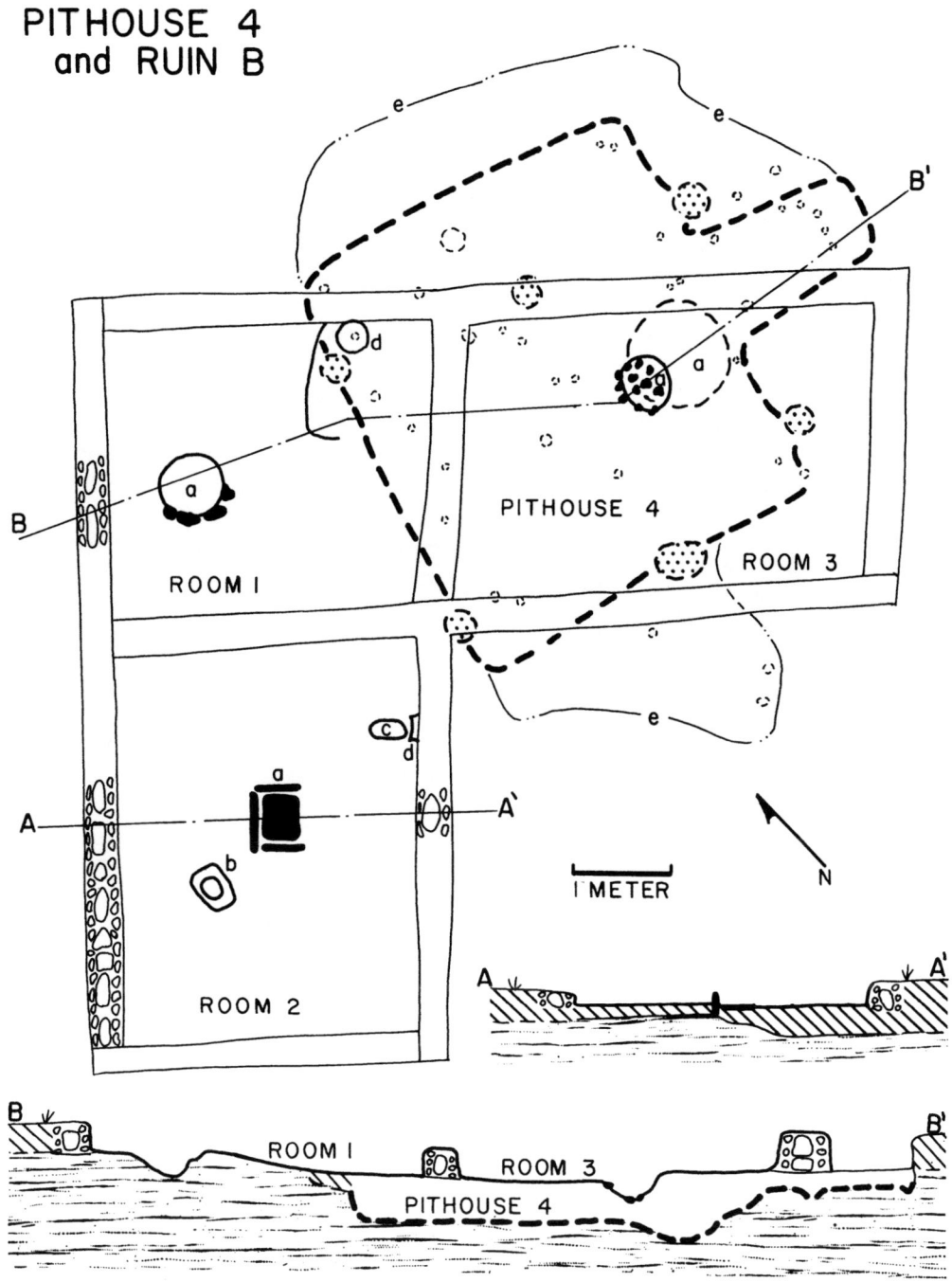

Fig. 6. Plan and sections of Pithouse 4 and Ruin B. Horizontal streak, native clay; hatching, trash; black, rock; stipple, main postholes; *a*, hearths; *b*, metate; *c*, grinding slab; *d*, sherds plastered in floor and wall; *e*, limit of excavation. Unlettered features indicated by circles are secondary postholes.

Hearth: Circular clay basin, 1.00 m. in diameter.

Pits: None.

Postholes: Six main postholes; pair recessed into front and back walls; all but one main posthole contained ash. Numerous secondary postholes.

Material culture on floor: None recorded.

Remarks: This pithouse suffered from extreme rodent activity. Superposition of parts of two rooms of Ruin B accounts for much of the ceramic mixture. An adjacent "storage room" was postulated by the original excavator but evidence is not conclusive.

Pithouse 5

Illustrations: Figs. 7, 8.

Dimensions: North-south, 3.60 m.; east-west, 3.80 m. Depth from present surface, 0.75 m.

Walls: Bottom of walls formed by pit excavated into native clay. Tuff boulders on native clay above the southwest corner are possibly the base for an upper wall of jacal. Shallow recess in the south wall opposite the entrance(?).

Entrance: Oriented towards north(?); stepped(?). Length, 0.70 m.; width, 0.55 m. Two possible ladder holes 0.45 m. apart and 0.50 m. from the south wall were inclined 10 to 15 degrees from vertical towards the hearth. If Pithouse 5 had a roof entry the postulated entrance may have been a ventilator(?).

Floor: Shallow concave floor of native clay. Plaster evidence only at perimeter of pithouse due to rodent action.

Hearth: Lined with sandstone and tuff cobbles; earlier firepit dug into native clay beneath.

Pits: Three deep, over 0.28 m., sub-floor storage pits; on the basis of the fill sherds the circular pit in the east end of the pithouse is believed to be the result of the subsequent occupation. (See discussion on p. 59.) Three shallow, under 0.28 m., floor pits were noted. Two pits occur outside the pithouse walls.

Postholes: All six main support postholes recessed into the walls; pair recessed into the front and back walls(?). Numerous secondary postholes. The easternmost recessed main posthole in the south wall had a plastered section suggesting that the recessed roof support was plastered into the posthole to make it flush with the wall. The plaster was 5 cm. below floor level and parallel to the plane of the wall.

Material culture on floor: 4 manos and handstones, 2 metates, 3 hammerstones, 3 abrading stones, 2 blades-saws, 2 cores, 2 choppers, 1 Pine Flat Neck Corrugated jar, 1 Alma Smudged bowl.

Remarks: The pithouse depression was subsequently occupied. (Discussed further on p. 59.) Entry designation not definite. Roof entrance is postulated on the basis of the possible ladder holes near the south wall. The alternative of a possible north entry is based on placement of a notch in the north wall in relation to postholes and hearth, as suggested by other Nantack Phase pithouses. Four charcoal specimens from the floor fill were not datable.

Pithouse 6

Illustrations: Figs. 9, 10.

Dimensions: North-south, 4.20 m.; east-west, 3.50 m. Depth from present surface, average, 1.00 m.

Walls: Bottom of walls formed by pit ex-

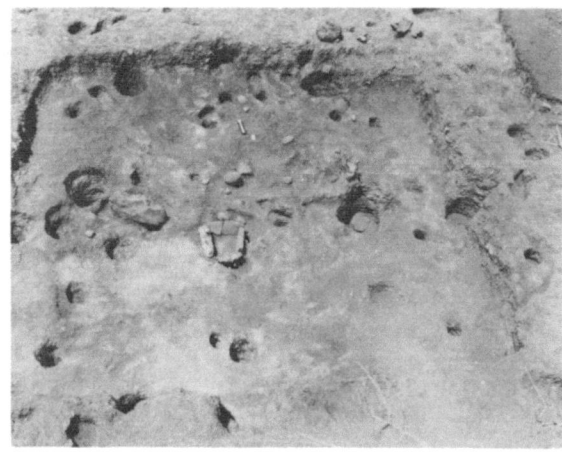

Fig. 7. Pithouse 5. The short trench out from pithouse wall in the foreground is possibly an entryway.

THE NANTACK PHASE

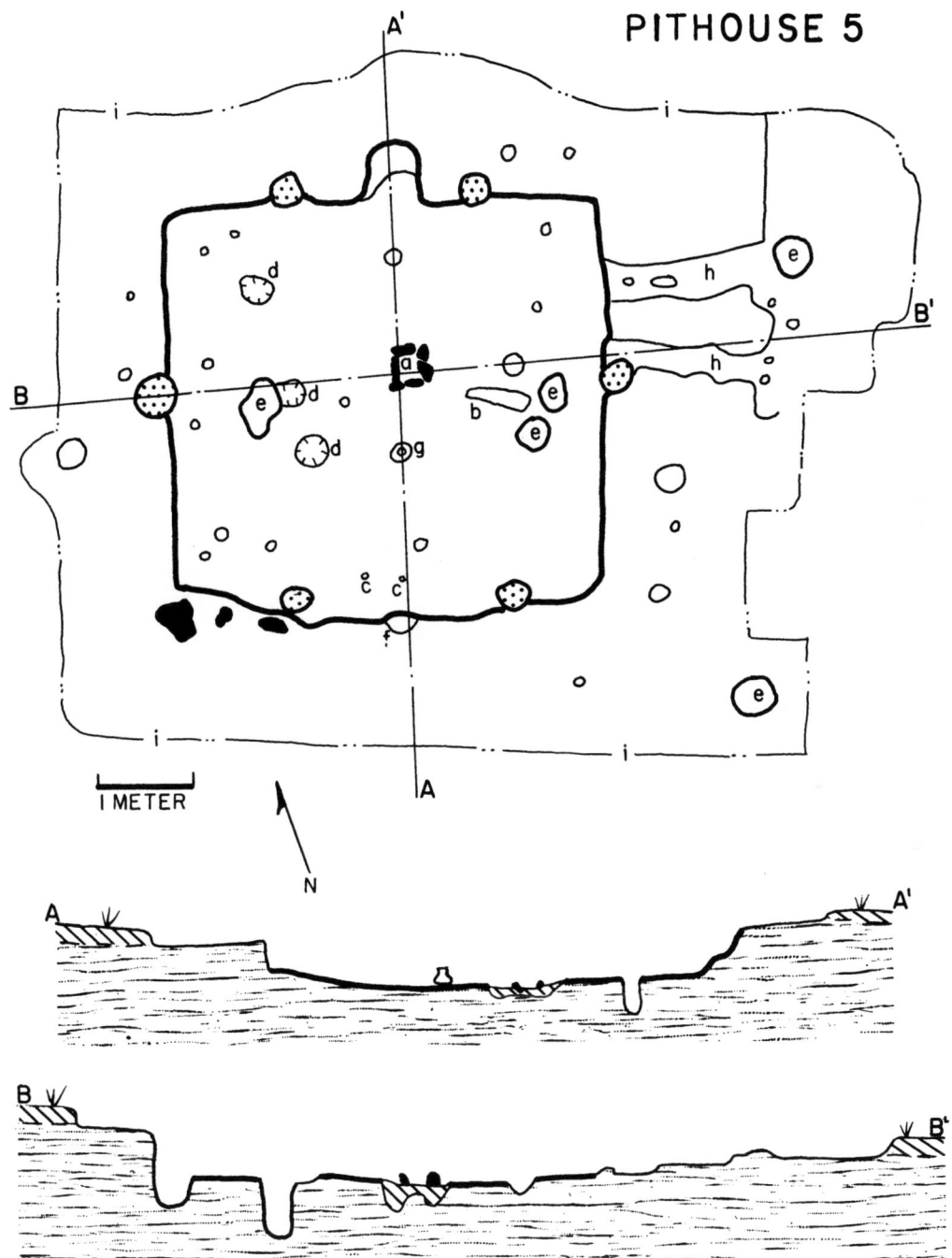

Fig. 8. Plan and sections of Pithouse 5. Horizontal streak, native clay; hatching, trash; black, rock; stipple, main postholes; *a*, hearth; *b*, metate; *c*, ladder holes(?); *d*, shallow floor depressions; *e*, deep storage pits; *f*, wall recess; *g*, Pine Flat Neck Corrugated jar; *h*, passageways(?)-ventilators(?); *i*, limit of excavation. Unlettered features indicated by circles are secondary postholes.

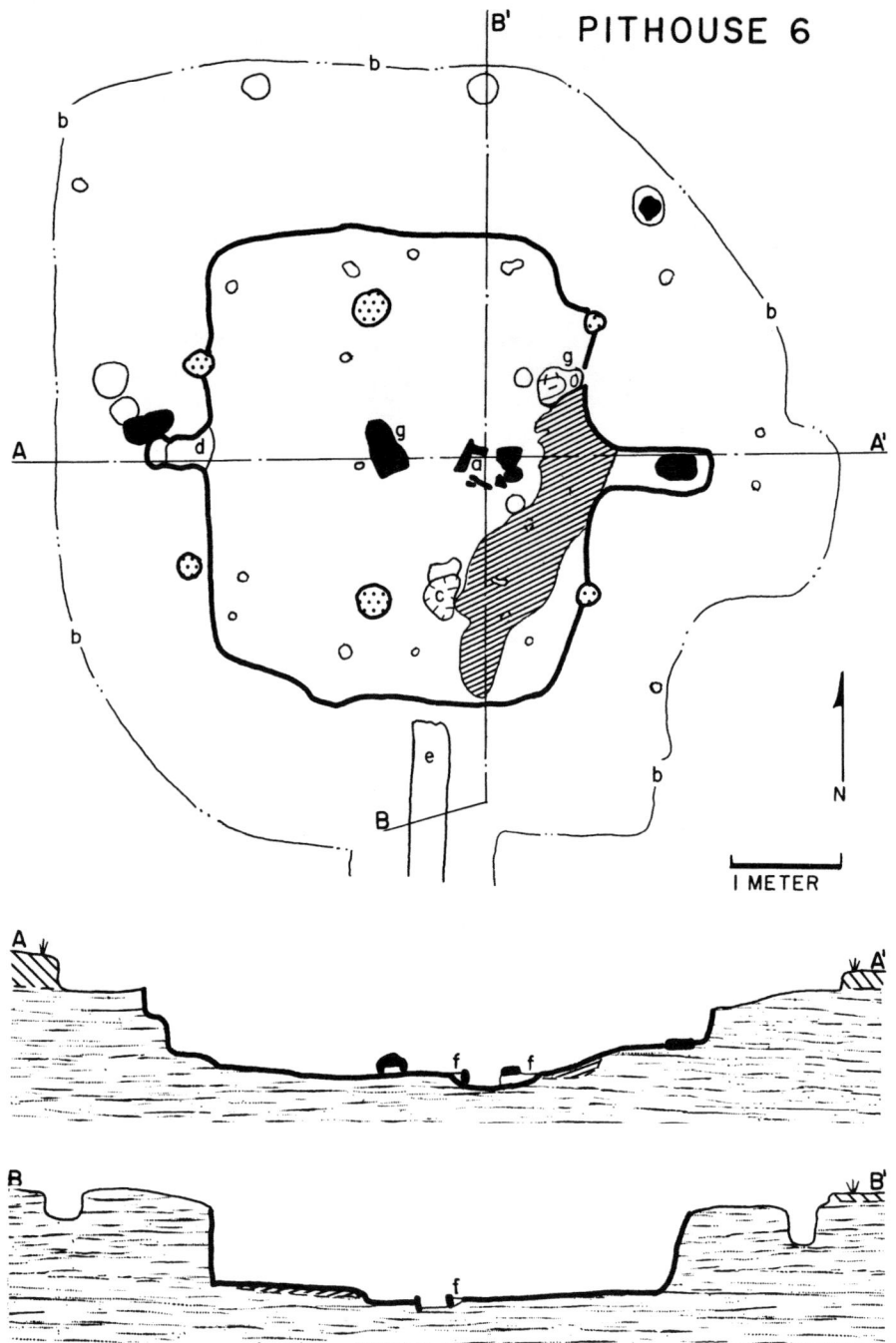

Fig. 9. Plan and sections of Pithouse 6. Horizontal streak, native clay; wide hatching, trash; narrow hatching, floor plaster; stipple, main postholes; *a*, hearth; *b*, limit of excavation; *c*, shallow floor depression; *d*, wall recess; *e*, footing trench(?); *f*, ash; *g*, metates. Unlettered features indicated by circles are secondary postholes.

cavated into native clay. Plaster preserved behind "Utah" metate near entrance. Recess in west wall, opposite entrance, two-stepped; ventilator(?).

Entrance: Oriented towards east; ramp with terminal step. Length, 1.00 m.; width, 0.30 m. Slab found at the eastern end, on walking surface.

Floor: Plaster preserved around the entrance and hearth areas.

Hearth: Rock outlined, no ash present. Underlying firepit dug into native clay contained ash.

Pits: One shallow floor depression in southeast quadrant.

Postholes: Six main support postholes; two single postholes in line with pair of recessed postholes in front and back walls. Several secondary postholes. Remodeling indicated by secondary postholes under floor plaster.

Material culture on floor: 10 manos and handstones, 5 metates, 1 perforated sherd, 1 projectile point, 2 Pine Flat Neck Corrugated jars, 1 Alma Scored jar.

Remarks: The pithouse depression was subsequently occupied. (See p. 60.)

PITHOUSE 8

Illustrations: Figs. 11, 12.
Dimensions: North-south, 3.70 m.; east-west, 4.05 m.(?). Depth from present surface, 0.55 to 0.90 m.

Walls: Bottom of walls formed by pit excavated into native clay. Due to the natural slope of the ridge the west wall is 0.55 m. deep into the native clay and the east side of the pithouse only 0.15 m. deep.

Entrance: Not definitely located. Placement of the recessed postholes and the hearth are basis for postulating that the entry is in the center of the north wall and subsequently obliterated by a storage pit.

Floor: Plaster over all of the floor(?), but indistinct on the downhill (east) side.

Hearth: Circular, rock-lined; built over depression in native clay.

Pits: One definite sub-floor storage pit partly recessed into south wall. Eight pits and depressions around the perimeter of the pithouse. (See section on Pits Outside Houses.)

Postholes: Six(?) main postholes; pair of main postholes recessed into north and south walls; two(?) single main support posts. Numerous secondary postholes. Neither of the two secondary postholes recessed into the west wall extend below floor level.

Material culture on floor: 13 manos and handstones; 1 metate, 1 grinding slab, 3 hammerstones,

FIG. 10. Pithouse 6. The straight trench at the top of the pithouse wall to the left of the meter bar is the "footing trench."

FIG. 11. Pithouse 8. The floor pit at the side of the entrance to the Great Kiva is shown in the upper right hand corner.

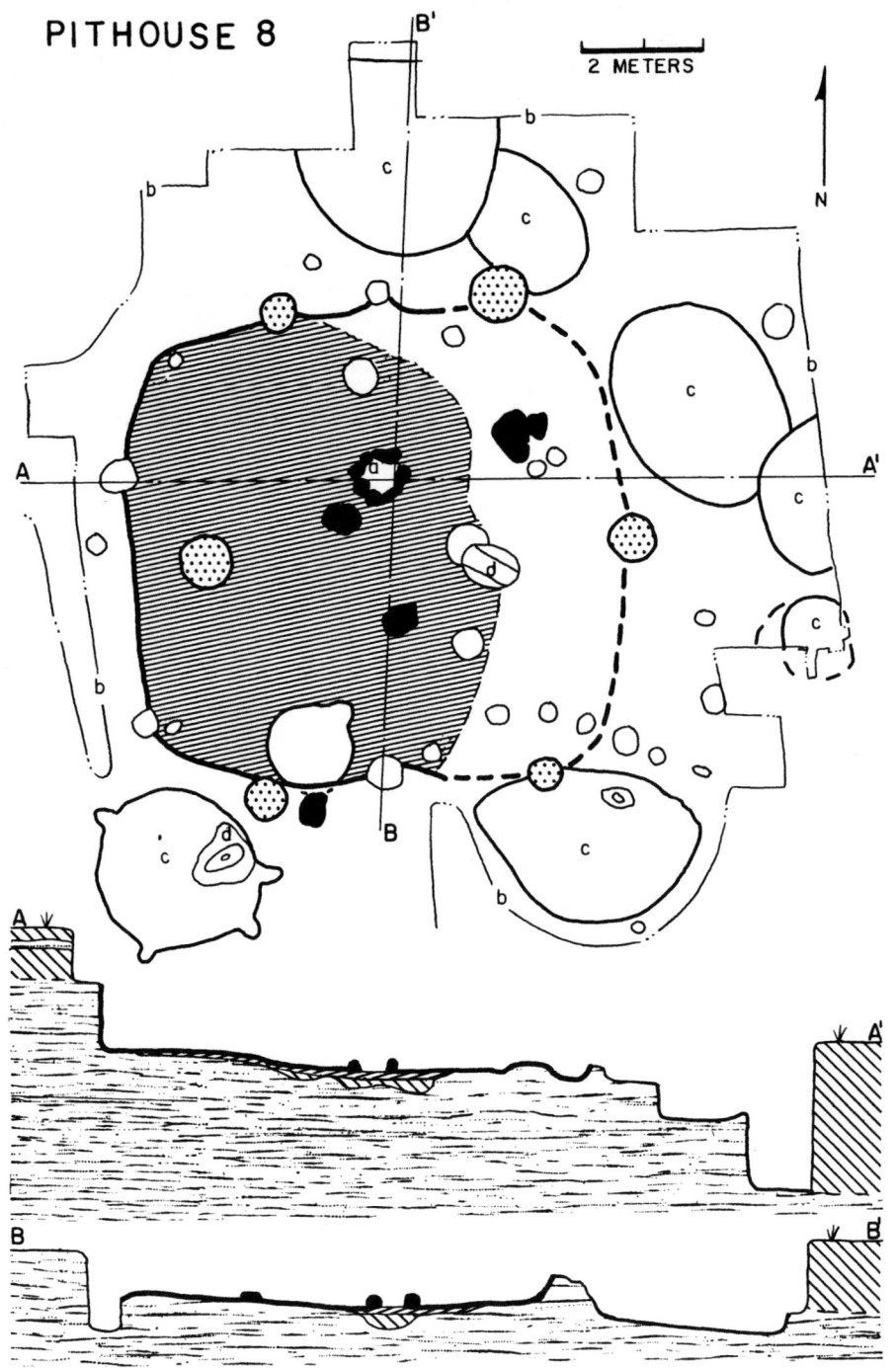

Fig. 12. Plan and sections of Pithouse 8. Horizontal streak, native clay; wide hatching, trash; black, rock; narrow hatching, floor plaster; stipple, main postholes; *a*, hearth; *b*, limit of excavation; *c*, storage pits; *d*, metates. Unlettered features indicated by circles are secondary postholes.

1 maul, 7 Three Circle Neck Corrugated jars, 2 Alma Plain jars, 1 Alma Scored jar, 1 Alma Plain pitcher, 1 Pine Flat Neck Corrugated jar, 1 Mangas Black-on-white jar.

Remarks: The location of the east wall is postulated on the basis of the dimensions of other Nantack Phase pithouses, the natural slope of the hill, the location of material culture on the floor, and the positioning of the adjacent subsurface pits. Two charred juniper logs on the floor indicate that Pithouse 8 burned. This structure is built at the side of the Great Kiva entrance and is younger than the ceremonial unit.

PITHOUSE 9

Illustrations: Fig. 1.

Dimensions: North-south, across "back wall," 4.30 m. Depth from present surface, average, 1.25 m. Although incompletely excavated indications are that this unit was rectangular.

Walls: Bottom of walls formed by pit dug into native clay. Exposed wall 65 to 75 cm. deep into native clay. Recess in center of west (back) wall.

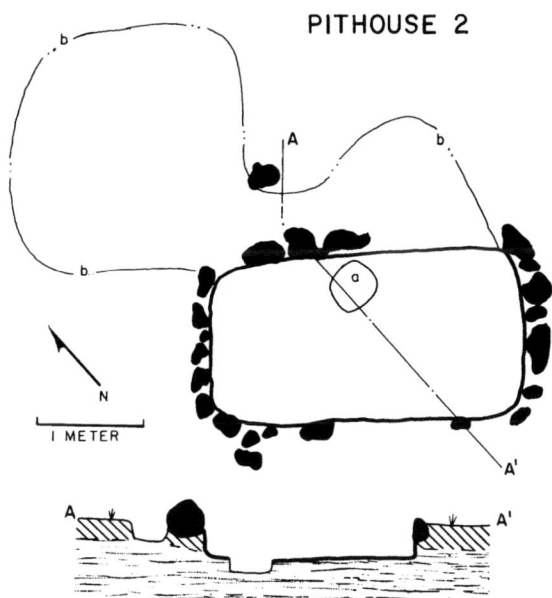

FIG. 13. Plan and section of Pithouse 2. Horizontal streak, native clay; hatching, trash; black, rock; *a*, hearth; *b*, limit of excavation.

Entrance: Not located; possibly to east.

Floor: Thinly plastered on native clay floor; very smooth.

Hearth: Not located.

Pits: One, 0.17 m. deep oblong floorpit.

Postholes: Pair of postholes recessed into west wall. Eight secondary postholes.

Material culture on floor: 1 fragmentary Alma Smudged bowl, 1 mano fragment.

Remarks: Pithouse 9 was located under the trash mound at the northern end of the side. It was not completely excavated but several features indicate that this is a Nantack Phase dwelling. These features include: the ceramic complex; the pair of recessed postholes in the west (back?) wall and the recess (ventilator?) which occur in Pithouses 5(?) and 6. The entension of floor plaster on fill in the eastern portion of the trash mound trench is probably the pithouse entrance.

HOUSE WITH NO LATERAL ENTRY

PITHOUSE 2

Illustrations: Fig. 13.

Dimensions: Length, 2.70 m.; width, average, 1.50 m. Depth from present surface, 0.60 m.

Walls: Bottom of walls formed by pit cut into native clay. Most of the wall perimeter outlined with boulders of tuff and basalt, including metate fragments. Over a cubic meter of rock was taken from the fill and indicates that the above surface walls were at least partly rock.

Entrance: None found.

Floor: Irregular native clay.

Hearth: The shallow depression near the north wall was burned.

Pits: None.

Postholes: None.

Material culture on floor: None.

Remarks: This structure does not resemble any of the other Nantack Phase pithouses at Nantack Village. Its small size, lack of artifacts, and indications of above ground rock walls have led to the postulations that Pithouse 2 was used as a storage unit, woman's house or sweat lodge. Assignment to the Nantack Phase is tenuous.

Unclassified House
Pithouse 7

Illustrations: Fig. 14.

Dimensions: Maximum extent of excavation about 6.00 by 3.30 m. Depth from present surface, average, 0.68 m.

Walls: Pit dug into slope of native clay hill; indefinite and shallow with much rodent activity.

Entrance: None located.

Floor: Irregular native clay.

Hearth: None located.

Pits: One pit, 0.40 m. deep, within limits of excavation.

Postholes: Eight small holes in the floor were designated postholes; there is no pattern and the extensive rodent activity may have accounted for some of them.

Material culture on floor: 1 circular basin metate.

Remarks: Pithouse 7 is both eroded and indistinct, overlain by Ruin C, Room 2 and dug into the ridge slope. Although Pithouse 7 is not like other Nantack Phase dwelling units there is no evidence that it is not a Nantack Phase structure.

Ceremonial Structures
Great Kiva

Illustrations: Figs. 15, 16.

Dimensions: North-south, average, 10.75 m.; east-west, 13.0 m.(?). Depth from present surface, west wall, 1.15 m.; east end, 0.15 m.

Walls: Dug into ridge slope. Lower portion of wall formed by native clay; no evidence of upper wall construction.

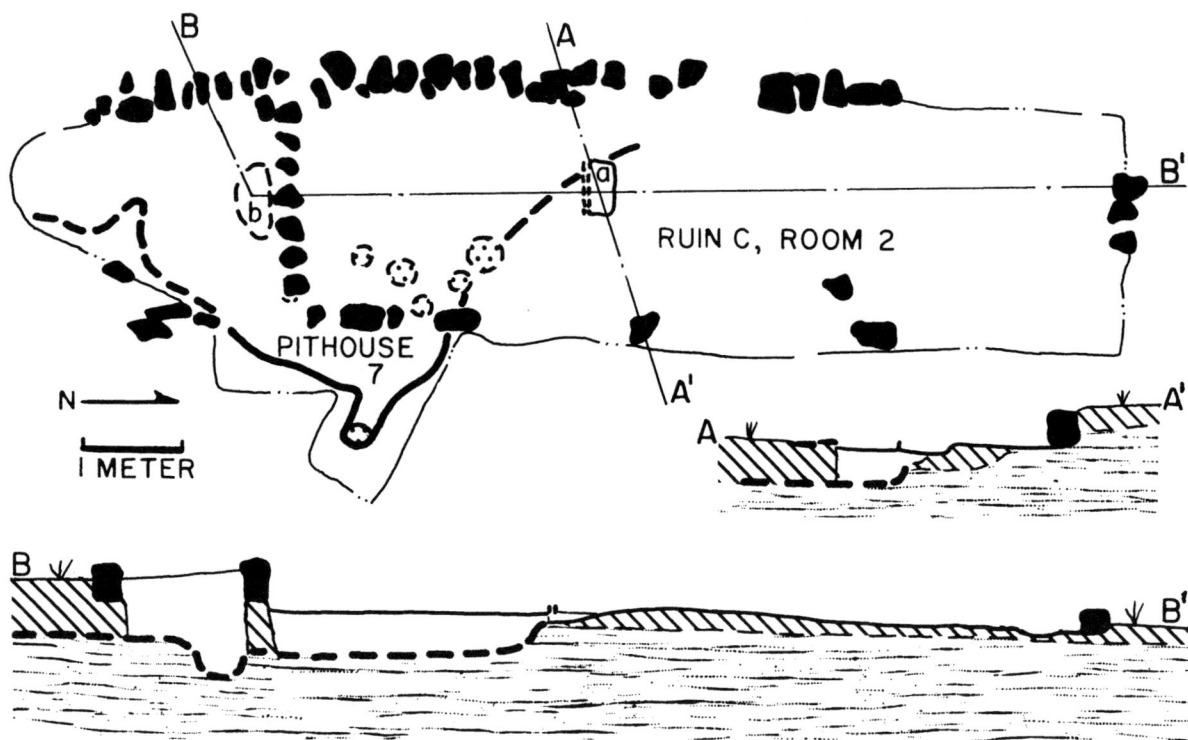

Fig. 14. Plan and sections of Pithouse 7 and Ruin C, Room 2. Horizontal streak, native clay; hatching, trash; stipple, postholes; *a*, hearth; *b*, storage pit; *c*, limit of excavation.

Entrance: Length, 2.25 m.(?); width, 5.80 m.(?). The eastern entrance is broad and access to the Great Kiva gained by first stepping up onto a partly artificial rise of native clay.

Floor: Spots of plaster over native clay removed during excavation. Floor damaged by rodent activity, especially in the west end. A shallow trench 4.50 meters long in the northwest corner is attributed to subsequent occupation.

Hearth: Not definitely located. The shallow depression north of the central posthole contained a mixture of native soil and ash; the orange floor of this depression indicates exposure to heat or fire.

Pits: Two floor pits near the entrance contain metates and are 0.30 m. and 0.40 m. deep. Both are thought to be intrusive into the Great Kiva subsequent to its period of active use. Burial 4

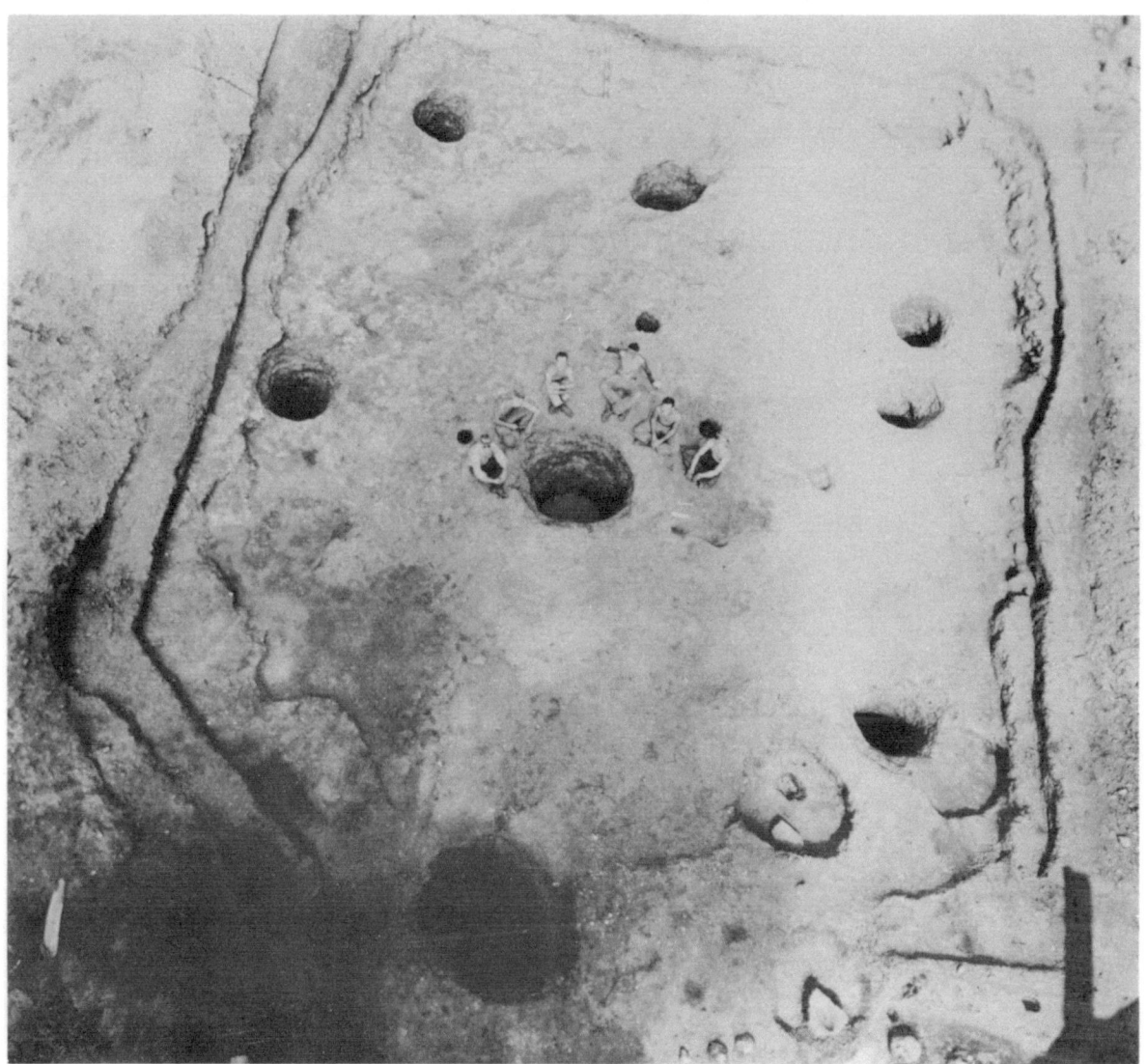

Fig. 15. The Great Kiva. The meter bar is against the back (west) wall. The sharp shadow line around the Great Kiva is the limit of excavation and not the wall.

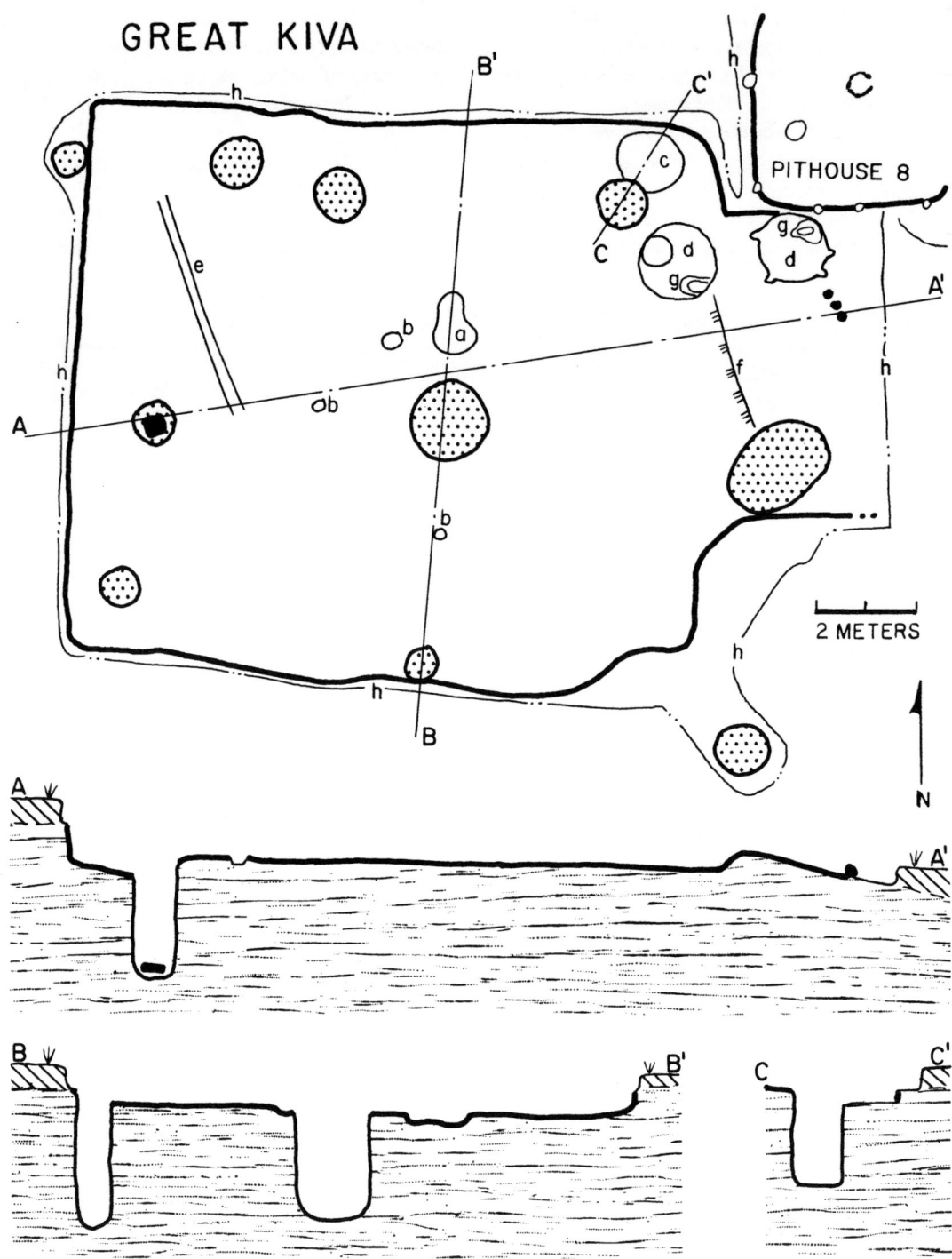

Fig. 16. Plan and sections of Great Kiva. Horizontal streak, native clay; hatching, trash; black, rock; stipple, main postholes; *a*, hearth(?); *b*, secondary postholes; *c*, warming basin(?); *d*, floor pits; *e*, floor trench; *f*, clay step; *g*, metates; *h*, limit of excavation.

was recovered from a pit within one of the floor pits. The shallow depression in the northeast corner was filled with six dozen fire-cracked rocks and is perhaps a warming oven or basin.

Postholes: Placement of the ten large main support postholes indicates an asymmetrical roofing arrangement. Their great size is distinctive. The majority had wedge boulders in the upper part of the posthole fill. The original post was in place in the deep central posthole. This posthole is 1.50 m. in diameter but the post only about 0.60 m. in diameter and wedged in place by boulders between the post and the posthole wall. The large diameter of the main support postholes is thought to be the by-product of the depth, the proportion of these measurements being consistent. The main posthole near the center of the west wall had a sandstone footing slab at the bottom. Three secondary postholes are in a semi-circle around the central posthole.

Material culture on floor: 1 each mano fragment, abrading stone and hammerstone; 2 metates and 1 mano from the floor pits.

Remarks: Floor area of the Great Kiva is 152.8 square meters as compared to an average of 16.2 square meters for Pithouses 1, 3, 4, 5, 6, and 8. Towards the east end the walls are very shallow and hard to trace due to the natural slope of the ridge. The southeast corner has the shallowest walls and does not entirely conform in plan to the rest of the Great Kiva. There is, however, no evidence that the posthole shown outside the walls was ever within the structure proper. There is evidence that at least a portion of the Great Kiva stood open after it had fallen into disuse. The posthole northeast of the northern end of the shallow floor trench had a layer of washed plaster about 0.45 m. below the floor. This is interpreted as floor and wall plaster which washed into the posthole as the timber disintegrated.

Pithouse 10

Illustrations: Figs. 17, 18.

Note: This semi-subterranean unit is not definitely proved to be a ceremonial structure but is classified as such on the basis of its size and the presence of the sub-floor trench.

Dimensions: North-south, 7.50 m.; east-west, 8:00 m. Depth from present surface, average, 0.75 m.

Walls: Bottom of walls formed by pit excavated into native clay. In good condition except at northwest corner where it is discontinuous and in the northeast corner where there has been tree root disturbance.

Entrance: None located. Possibly through northwest corner.

Floor: Native clay; rodent activity around west wall and near sub-floor trench.

Hearth: None located.

Pits: Four within pithouse walls. Three are apparently storage pits and the fourth, in the northwest corner, is possibly a warming basin or oven. Less than a dozen fire-cracked rocks were taken from this depression but the native clay has been subjected to heat or fire. The remaining three pits are discussed in the section on Pits Outside Houses.

Sub-floor trench: Trench 3.08 by 0.53 m. with enlarged, circular ends located in the western half of the structure. Its sides are vertical and two small postholes(?) on either side suggest a floor drum. There is no evidence that the trench was used for storage.

Postholes: Seven main support postholes are recessed into the walls; three main postholes are not recessed. The majority of the numerous secondary postholes are recessed.

Material culture on floor: 3 manos, 1 metate, 1 miniature bowl.

Remarks: Ceramic evidence indicates that Pithouse 10 is younger than the Great Kiva. If this is a Nantack Phase unit it is late in the phase. There is a possibility that it is associated with the surface units at the north end of the site. It is postulated that the trash mound over Pithouse 9 was formed as a result of the construction of Pithouse 10.

Pits Outside House

Pithouse 1 (Fig. 2). A storage pit is located outside the south corner of the pithouse; diameter, 1.05 m.; depth, into native clay, 0.85 m.; slightly

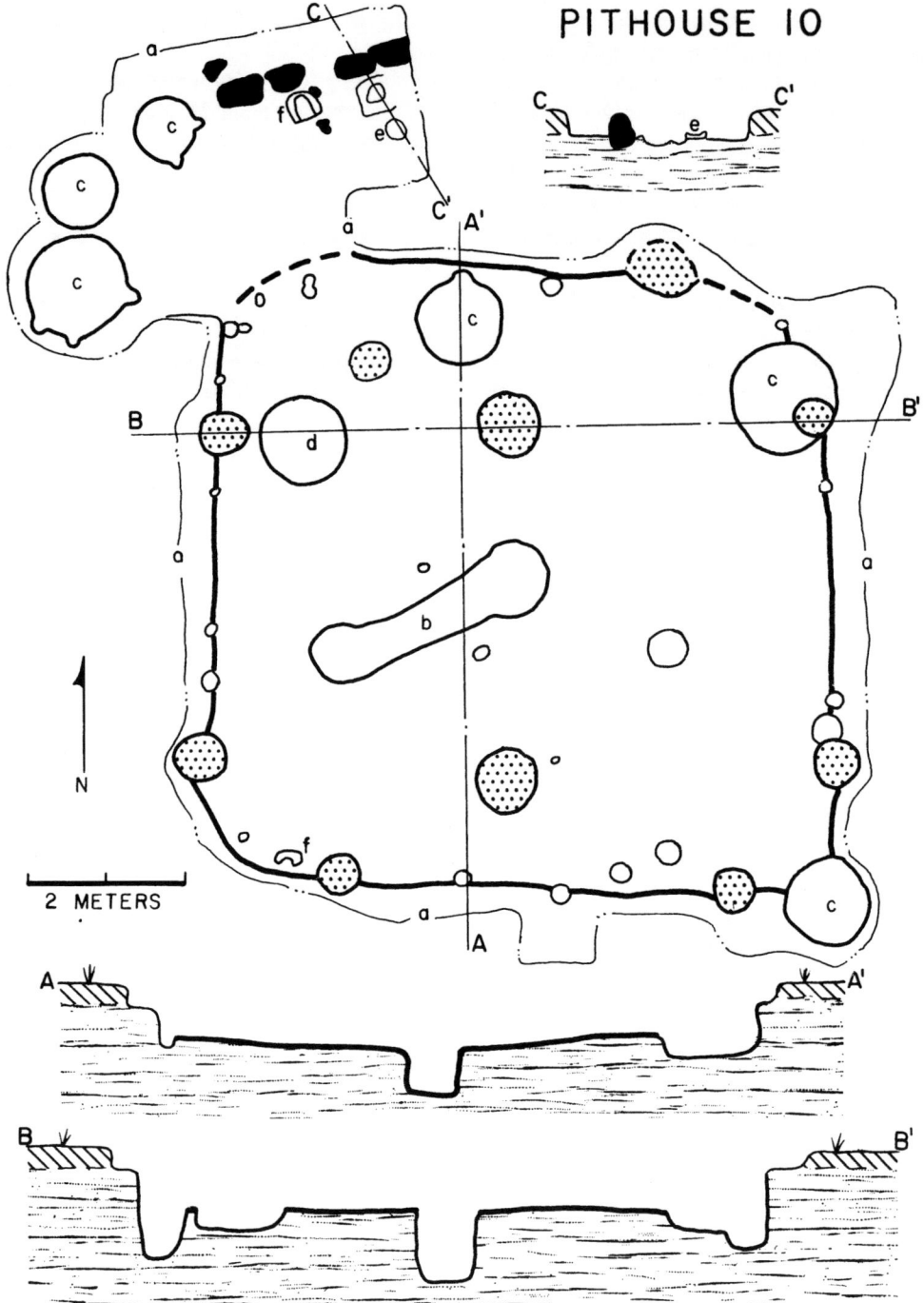

Fig. 17. Plan and sections of Pithouse 10. Horizontal streak, native clay; hatching, trash; black, rock; stipple, main postholes; *a*, limit of excavation; *b*, sub-floor trench; *c*, storage pits; *d*, warming basin(?); *e*, ash; *f*, metate. Unlettered features indicated by circles are secondary postholes.

Fig. 18. Pithouse 10.

bell-shaped; potsherds and stone artifacts in fill; maul on floor. There are three postholes at intervals around the pit and they may have been for roofing, but there is no conclusive proof that this pit was a functional part of Pithouse 1. Alma Plain, Black River Variety sherds in the storage pit fill give some credence to the possibility that the pit antedates the occupation of Pithouse 1.

Pithouse 5 (Fig. 8). One deep and one shallow sub-surface pit lie to the east of Pithouse 5. A few potsherds are the only material culture found in these pits.

Pithouse 8 (Fig. 12). One pit, containing a worn out basin metate, is within the walls of the Great Kiva and appears to be intrusive. It is 0.30 m. deep and 1.30 m. in diameter. Four peripheral notches or postholes suggest that this pit had a covering or superstructure, but there is no evidence that it was roofed with Pithouse 8.

Four of the depressions or recesses around the eastern and northern end of Pithouse 8 are dug less than 0.28 m. deep into native clay. They were not found until the pithouse was completely excavated and it is not possible to determine their original depth or the surface from which they were dug. None contained more than a few potsherds.

Two pits east of the pithouse were over 0.40 m. deep; one was bell-shaped and the other contained two metate fragments. The large shallow pit on the north side of Pithouse 8 may have been cut through the entrance and accordingly postdates the pithouse occupation.

Pithouse 10 (Figs. 17, 18). Northwest of Pithouse 10 are three pits over 0.28 m. deep. One pit contained 15 potsherds, the others less than a half dozen. Two pits have peripheral notches or postholes, again suggesting a covering or superstructure.

Summary. The 13 pits outside the pithouse walls have the following characteristics:

Deep (over 0.28 m.) 8
Shallow (under 0.28 m.) 5
Peripheral notches 3
Bell-shaped 2

There is no record of adjacent sub-surface pits which have been roofed as a functional part of dwelling units in the Mogollon Culture area. If the presence of peripheral notches indicates a superstructure for these pits it is thought that they were separate from the dwellings.

Random, subsurface pits are a typical feature of the Mogollon Culture. The pits at Nantack Village may be thought of as storage features.

DISCUSSION

Table 1 shows the architectural characteristics of the semi-subterranean units excavated at Nantack Village. Comparison with Tables 5 and 6 in Wheat (1955) shows a good correlation of Nantack Village architectural features with other Mogollon 4 sites. This similarity is even more striking when Nantack Village pithouses are compared with features found in Mogollon 3 and 5 (Wheat 1955: 52, Table 4).

Dwelling units are rectangular in all cases where shape is known. The "quadrangular" pithouse with a lateral entryway is the typical dwelling unit in Mogollon 4 (Wheat 1955: 49). Walls are either straight-sided or slightly outcurving.

Peripheral rocks occur in four dwellings and they are assumed to be for the basal support of jacal walls. This rock base may represent the beginning of the transition from semi-subterranean pithouses to surface, masonry dwellings. Surface, masonry dwellings begin at A.D. 1000, the Reserve Phase, in the Point of Pines region.

The floors were undoubtedly clay plastered, and plastering over of secondary postholes in Pithouses 1, 6, and 8 may suggest remodeling or reoccupation.

Main support postholes recessed in pairs is a consistent pattern. Placement of the six, and in one case seven, main postholes speaks well for a postulated low gable or flat roof.

The hearth is rock-lined in four of the seven pithouses with a definite firebox. At Nantack Village this is a departure from the usual pattern of simple, unlined clay fire pits usually found in Mogollon 4 sites (Wheat 1955: 51). However, in each of the four cases there is a clay-lined firepit underlying the rock-lined hearth. Hearths are typically located between the foot of the entrance and the geographical center of the pithouse.

Artifacts on the floor are primarily of a domestic nature, such as metates, manos and handstones, hammerstones, and ceramic vessels.

Sub-surface pits outside the pithouse walls have been discussed and summarized previously. Intramural storage pits occur in four pithouses.

The one definite and the other possible ceremonial structure deserve mention. Two units, the Great Kiva and Pithouse 10, have the following features in common:

Larger than the dwelling units
Rectangular
Possible warming basin or oven
10 post roof support pattern different from domestic structures

The sub-floor trench in Pithouse 10 is the most distinctive floor feature not associated with the dwelling units. Size has already been mentioned as differing from domestic structures. The location of Pithouse 10 at the extreme northeastern end of the site in the largest level area on the ridge provides additional evidence for the suggestion that the structure is ceremonial in nature.

The Great Kiva is the largest single Mogollon structure which has been completely excavated, on the basis of over-all floor area (Wheat 1955, Table 6). The extremely large postholes indicate an asymmetrical roofing pattern and suggest a flat roof. The wide, elevated step entry is not seen in any other units at Nantack Village. Wide, stepped kiva entrances occur in the Forestdale Valley in the 12th century (Haury 1950: 38). The Great Kiva is not obviously similar to any of the five other excavated ceremonial structures assigned to the Mogollon 4 period (Wheat 1955: 60, Table 6). However, the lack of a defined architectural pattern is given as a characteristic of kivas during the 900–1000 period in the

TABLE 1. ARCHITECTURAL CHARACTERISTICS OF SEMI-SUBTERRANEAN STRUCTURES

Characteristics	Pithouses										Great Kiva
	1	2	3	4	5	6	7	8	9	10	
Shape											
Rectangular	x	x	x	x	x	x		x	?	x	x
Indeterminate							x				
Floor Area in Square Meters (to nearest whole number)	18	4	21	15	14	15		15		60	153
Entrance											
Ramp with terminal step	x										
Stepped	?		x	x	?			x		x	Elevated step
Oriented North					?			?			
Oriented Northeast			x				x		x		
Oriented East				x		x			?		x
Oriented Southeast	x										
Roof entry					?						
Not located		x					x	x	x	x	
Wall Features											
Recess opposite entry					?	x			?		
Wall niche	x										
Peripheral rocks	x	x			x			x			
Plaster evidence			x			x			x		
Floor Features											
Catch basin	x										
Warming basin or oven										?	?
Plaster evidence	x		x	x	x	x	x	x	x	x	x
Hearth											?
Clay-lined	x	x	x		x	x		x			
Rock-lined	x				x	x		x			
Sub-hearth depression										x	
Not located							x		x		
Pits											
Within pithouse walls					6		1	1	1	3	2
Outside pithouse walls	1				2			7		3	2
Shallow (under 0.28 m.)					4			3		1	
Deep (over 0.28 m.)	1				4		1	5		5	2
Main Support Postholes											
Recessed	x		x	x	x	x		x	x	x	1 of 10
Recessed in pairs	x		x	x	x	x		?	x	x	
6 main supports			x	x	x	x		?			
7 main supports	x										
10 main supports											x
Burning					x	x		x		x	
Remodeling or Reoccupation	x		x		x			x			x

Mogollon area. Artifacts with a domestic connotation are lacking from the floor of the Great Kiva.

RELATIVE DATING
Pithouse 1 is older than Pithouse 5
The Great Kiva is older than Pithouse 8
Pithouse 9 is older than Pithouse 10
Pithouse 4 is older than any of the rooms in Ruin B
Pithouse 7 is older than Ruin C, Room 2

POTTERY

Potsherds were classified in the field and representative sherds saved for reanalysis in the laboratory. In the field sherds were segregated for each excavation level and architectural unit. In the laboratory combinations of field excavation units were made which would show ceramic relationships most significantly. Summary sherd tabulations are shown in Tables 2–4. Detailed sherd tabulations are available in Breternitz (1956).

The 50,768 potsherds from pithouse units, the Great Kiva, and burials may be classified as follows:

	Frequency	Number
Plainware	68.7%	34,895
Redware	15.3%	7,775
Textured Pottery	10.9%	5,506
Painted and intrusive pottery	5.1%	2,592
	100.0%	50,768

Typological designation of ceramic "varieties" follows Wheat, Gifford and Wasley (1958).

PLAINWARE

Alma Plain, Point of Pines Variety (Wheat 1954: 82). Most of the sherds from Nantack Village are locally-made Alma Plain. In the field sherds were not separated by variety and thus no sherd count based on varieties of Alma Plain can be reconstructed.

Vessel shapes are shown in Figure 19. Jars are globular with short necks and small mouths; orifice diameter, 11.0 to 15.2 cm.; maximum vessel diameter, 19.3 to 34.0 cm.; heights, 19.5 to 32.0 cm. Rim sherds indicate that bowls are deep and hemispherical. There are two sherds of bottle(?) vessels. One shallow dish (Fig. 19 c) is 10.1 cm. in maximum diameter and 2.0 cm. high. One pitcher (Fig. 19 b) is 10.5 cm. in both maximum diameter and height. Bowl-jar and seed jar vessels are indicated by rim sheds.

Within the Alma Plain category are seven sherds with teat-like applications of clay to the exterior. In the Reserve region this type is called Alma Knobby (Martin 1956: 155, 159).

Handles were recorded as follows: Strap, plain 11; strap, two-ribbed 7; strap, three-ribbed 5; lug, perforated 3; lug, plain 2; lug, knob 1.

Alma Plain, Black River Variety (Wheat 1954: 85). Represented by sherds from the fill of Pithouses 1, 2, 3, the Great Kiva, and the fill of the storage pit, Pithouse 1. In the latter case the vessel is a globular seed jar (Wheat 1954, Fig. 32 c). From the surface collection are several sherds from neck corrugated vessels with Alma Plain, Black River Variety paste.

Alma Smudged (Wheat 1954: 88). Vessel shapes, determined from 1151 sherds, correspond to those given by Wheat (1954, Fig. 33) with the exception of the bowl found with Burial 4. This vessel has a slightly recurved rim, is 14.5 cm. in maximum diameter, has an orifice diameter of 13.2 cm., and is 8.2 cm. high.

Alma Polished. These highly polished sherds of Alma Plain, Point of Pines Variety are an undescribed type. No vessel shape reconstructions could be made from the 706 sherds.

Alma Rough (Martin 1943: 238; Martin and Rinaldo 1940: 78). All 46 sherds of this type have local paste. Vessel shapes could not be determined.

Alma Textured Series (Haury 1936a: 38–40). This category includes *Alma Scored, Alma Incised* and *Alma Punched*. They are represented by 334, 14, and 45 sherds respectively and are made with local paste. Sherds indicate that vessel shapes fall within the range given in the original description.

Alma Grooved (Danson 1957: 87). The ex-

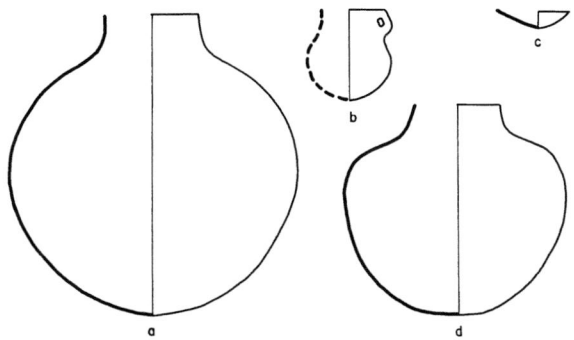

Fig. 19. Vessel shapes of Alma Plain, Point of Pines Variety. Maximum diameter of *a*, 34.5 cm.

terior of this undescribed type is grooved along coil junctures with a sharp, pointed tool. Both jar or pitcher and bowl shapes are represented by the 23 sherds recovered.

REDWARE

San Francisco Red, Point of Pines Variety (Wheat 1954: 88) and *Reserve Red, Point of Pines Variety* (Gifford 1957: 372–5). Both types occur at Nantack Village. Reserve Red is a development out of San Francisco Red and the diagnostic redware of the Nantack and Reserve phases at Point of Pines (Gifford 1957: 372). However, the presence of both at Nantack Village shows the contemporaneity, at least in part, of these two redware types. Macroscopically they both have local paste.

Jars range greatly in size but lack of whole vessels does not permit accurate measurements. Seed jars are indicated by rim sherds. Bowl forms fall within the range of shapes given by Wheat (1954, Fig. 34) and Gifford (1957: 374) except for one oblong-shaped Reserve Red bowl (Fig. 20 *b*).

One three-ribbed and four perforated lug handles were recorded.

San Francisco Red, Coiled Exterior (Martin, Rinaldo and Bluhm 1954: 73). Forty-six sherds have a coiled exterior often emphasized by grooving along coil junctures and nine sherds have a plain corrugated exterior. All sherds are from bowls and, macroscopically, have local paste.

San Francisco Red, Punched Exterior (Martin, Rinaldo and Bluhm 1954: 73). There are three bowl sherds of this type.

TEXTURED POTTERY

Alma Neck Banded (Haury 1936: 35). The local temper of tuff and gold-brown mica is present in all 66 sherds of this type. No sherds are on floor contact.

Three Circle Neck Corrugated, Point of Pines Variety. The 639 sherds and six restorable vessels fit Haury's description (1936a: 36) in all respects except paste, which is local. Shapes during the Nantack Phase are the same as for the Three Circle Phase (Fig. 21). Manipulation of the bottom neck coil by pinching, punching, or incising occurs in approximately 50% of the vessels. Some sherds with the bottom neck coil smoothed or rubbed to the extent that they are not recognizable as Three Circle Neck Corrugated, Point of Pines Variety are classified as Obliterated Neck Corrugated. Three Circle Neck Corrugated, Point of Pines Variety is a diagnostic type of the Nantack Phase.

NEW TYPE: PINE FLAT NECK CORRUGATED

Named For: Pine Flat Cave, San Carlos Apache Reservation, Arizona (Gifford 1957: 342).

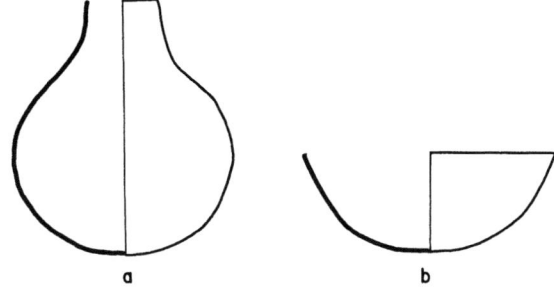

Fig. 20. Redware vessel shapes. *a*, San Francisco Red jar; *b*, Reserve Red bowl. Maximum diameter of *b*, 15.6 cm.

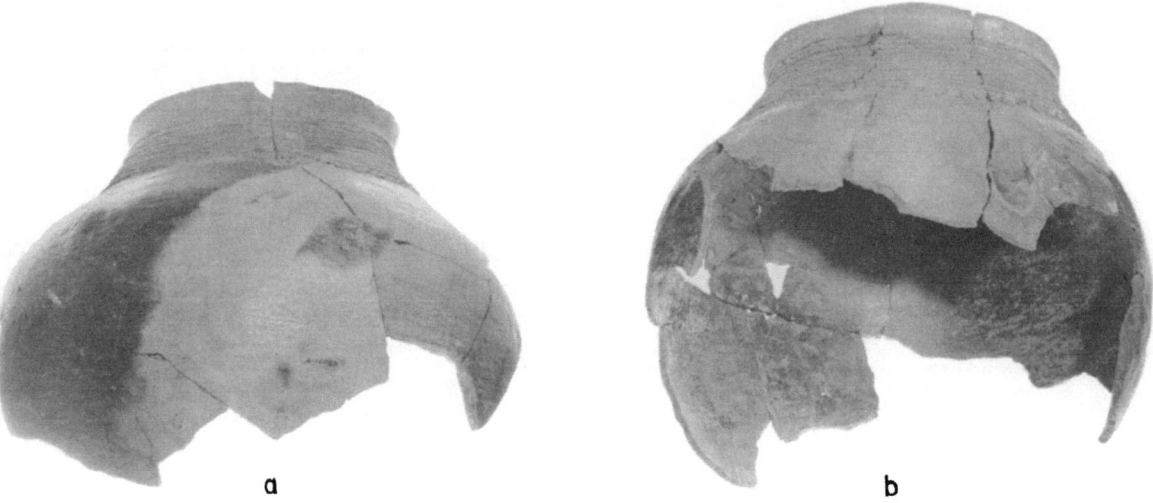

FIG. 21. Jars of Three Circle Neck Corrugated, Point of Pines Variety. Orifice diameter of *a*, 19.0 cm. Maximum diameter of *b*, 32.0 cm.

Previous Illustrations: Breternitz, Gifford and Olson 1957, Figure 3 *o*; Gifford 1957, Figures 133, 134 *a, c-g;* Haury 1957, Figure 14.

Type Specimens: Study collections at Arizona State Museum. Sherds AT 10574–10576 in Southwestern Ceramics Repository, Museum of Northern Arizona.

Type Site: Nantack Village, Arizona W: 10: 111.

Stage: Mogollon 4, Pueblo II.

Time: Ca. 850 to ca. 1050. Begins in Dry Lake Phase, is diagnostic of the Nantack Phase, and continues into the Reserve Phase.

Construction: Coiling followed by scraping.

Firing: Oxidizing atmosphere.

Paste: (a) *Color* — Reddish-brown through black. Majority with black core, probably due to firing technique. 2.5YR 5/8, 4/0; 5YR 5/6, 5/4, 5/1, 4/4, 3/1; 7.5YR 5/6, 5/4, 4/4, 4/0, 3/0; 10YR 3/1 (Munsell 1948). (b) *Temper* — Some angular to slightly rounded quartz grains and folia of gold-brown, inelastic mica. Moderately to well tempered. Fragments of whitish leucite tuff are more abundant than either mica or quartz but are inclusions in the clay and not added as temper. Temper usually of medium size with tuff particles frequently larger. (c) *Hardness* — 4.5 to 5.5. (d) *Fracture* — Irregular, often follows coils. Fracture surface rough and gritty but not crumbly.

Surface finish: Interiors scraped with occasional polishing marks parallel to the rim. Exteriors have variety of indentation techniques, which are always confined to jar necks. Ranges from wavy, indecisive indentations (Fig. 23 *b*) through a deeply indented, "imbricated" technique (Fig. 24 *a-e*) to a subindented, decorative technique (Fig. 24*f-i*). The "imbricated" technique is made by the thumb; the thumb nail is not used in the construction or decoration of the coil. The subindented, decorative technique is produced by the thumb nail and is confined to the bottom one-third to two-thirds of the coil. Nine neck corrugated sherds have the indentation produced by pinching the damp clay along coil junctures. One sherd is slipped red and thought to be a late variety. Rubbing over the indentations is most common on the lowest neck coils. Body sherds are indistinguishable from Alma Plain, Point of Pines Variety jar sherds. Mica flakes do not protrude and show on the surface in greater numbers than seen by core examination. (a) *Coils per 5 cm.*— 3 to 10; mode 5 (130 sherds). (b) *Indentations per 5 cm.* — 3 to 12; mode 7 (130 sherds).

Surface color: Exteriors light reddish-brown, through reddish-browns, to dark gray, 2.5YR 6/0, 5/6, 5/4, 5/0, 4/4; 5YR 6/6, 6/4, 5/6, 5/4, 5/3, 4/2, 4/1; 7.5YR 6/4, 5/4; 10YR 5/3, 5/1. Fire clouding not noted on textured areas. Interiors within the range of exterior color but usually a darker hue.

Form: Jars only. Globular jars with relatively short, slightly recurved necks are represented by only one complete vessel (Figs 23 a, 24 d). This vessel is 17.2 cm. high, 18.6 cm. in maximum diameter, and has a maximum orifice diameter of 11.1 cm. The majority of the vessels and diagnostic sherds have a relatively high and straight neck with a shallow shoulder (Fig. 23 b, 24 a-c). These larger jars have maximum orifice diameters up to 28.6 cm., maximum diameters up to 46.0 cm., and heights up to 45.7 cm. Two bowl-jar sherds are known.

Thickness of vessels at neck: Range 5 to 12 mm.; mode 7 to 8 mm. (130 sherds.)

Rims: Rounded.

Range: At present, known only from the Point of Pines region.

Remarks: Pine Flat Neck Corrugated differs from Three Circle Neck Corrugated in vessel shape, width of coils, and texturing technique. The "imbricated" technique closely resembles the textured surface of Elden Corrugated. Sherds which have been rubbed over the coils to the extent that they are not classifiable as Pine Flat Neck Corrugated are counted as Obliterated Neck Corrugated.

Cultural Association: Mogollon Culture, Black River Branch, Nantack Phase.

Reserve Incised Corrugated and *Reserve Punched Corrugated* (Rinaldo and Bluhm 1956: 162–7). These types are represented by 222 and

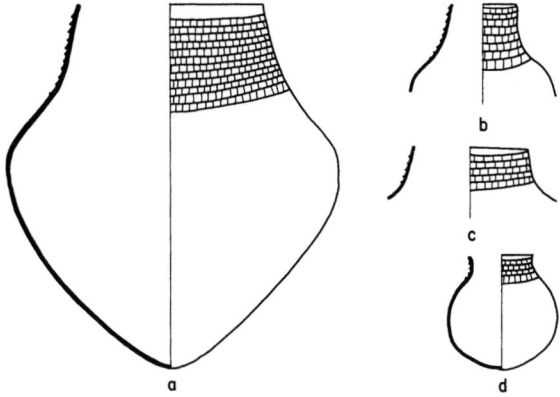

FIG. 22. Vessel shapes of Pine Flat Neck Corrugated. Maximum diameter of *a*, 46.0 cm.

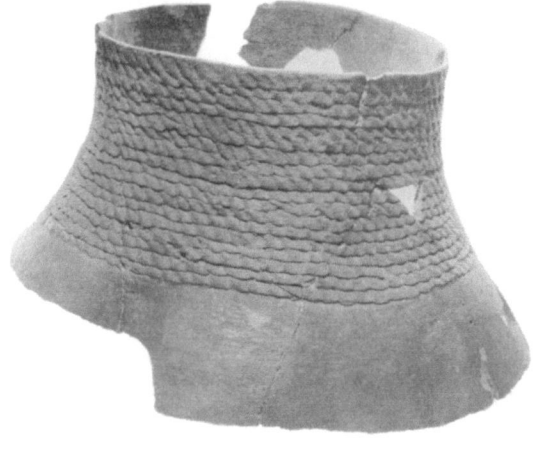

FIG 23. Jars of Pine Flat Neck Corrugated. Maximum diameter of *a*, 18.6 cm.; orifice diameter of *b*, 24.0 cm.

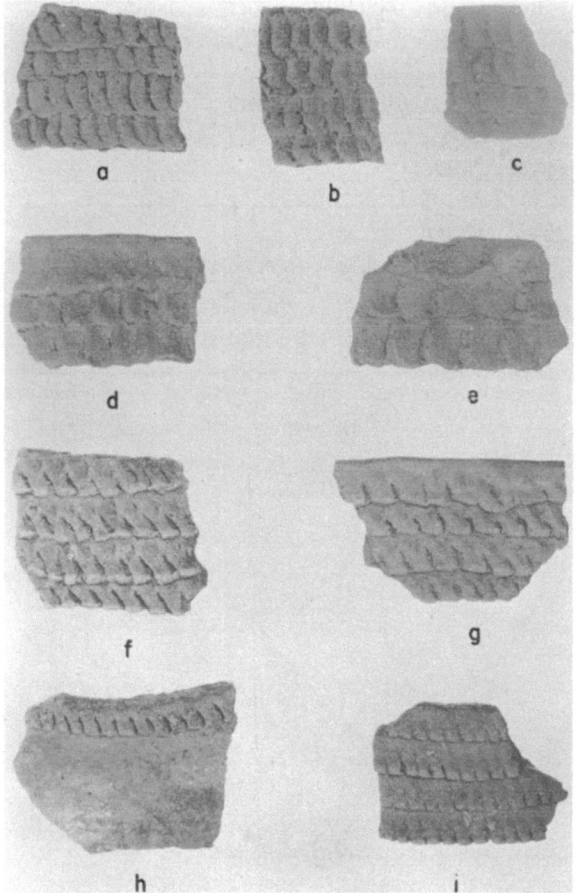

FIG. 24. Sherds of Pine Flat Neck Corrugated. Width of *h*, 7.3 cm.

30 sherds respectively. They are made with local paste and texturing is confined to the necks of jars, except in one case. There are 15 sherds in the Reserve Incised Corrugated category that are patterned by dragging a finger over the damp coils instead of using a tool to make the decoration.

Reserve Plain Corrugated and *Reserve Indented Corrugated* (Rinaldo and Bluhm 1956: 155–7), 159). These types are represented by 348 and 818 sherds respectively. They differ from the published descriptions only by virtue of being made with local paste. The Smudged Interior Varieties of both types (Rinaldo and Bluhm 1956: 157–61) are the smudged bowl forms and sometimes do occur at Nantack Village.

Plain Corrugated, Red Slipped and *Indented Corrugated, Red Slipped*. The 35 sherds of these types are given a descriptive name. They are diagnostic of post-Nantack phases in the Black River Branch and they will be described in subsequent reports.

Tularosa Patterned Corrugated (Rinaldo and Bluhm 1956: 169). This type and its variants of Smudged Interior and Reserve Variety are represented by 102 sherds. There are no sherds of this type on any of the pithouse floors.

Prieto Indented Corrugated (Breternitz, Gifford and Olson 1957, Fig 3 *c*). This type, called Alternating Indented Corrugated by Wendorf (1950: 38), is represented by eight sherds. It is a post-Nantack type in the Point of Pines region.

Point of Pines Obliterated Corrugated (Breternitz, Gifford and Olson 1957, Figs. 2, 3 *e*). None of the 225 of this post-Nantack type are from the floor and they are found only in the floor fill of Pithouse 10, the latest semi-subterranean unit at Nantack Village.

Point of Pines Punctate (Gifford 1957: 299–300). The six sherds represent the post-Nantack occupation of Nantack Village.

Reserve Fillet Rim (Martin and Rinaldo 1950a: 360). The one sherd recovered differs from Tularosa Fillet Rim by having plain instead of indented neck fillets.

Tularosa Fillet Rim (Wendorf 1950: 121). The 26 sherds of this post-Nantack type correspond to the local description.

McDonald Painted Corrugated, *McDonald Patterned Corrugated*, and *McDonald Grooved Corrugated* (Breternitz, Gifford and Olson 1957, Fig. 3 *f-h*). Represented by 12, 34 and nine sherds respectively, these types have been recognized as having temporal significance in the Point of Pines region. McDonald Painted Corrugated complies with the published description (Colton and Hargrave 1937: 61). McDonald Patterned Corrugated has white paint within the limits of a patterned corrugated decoration. McDonald Grooved Corrugated is a slipped redware with grooves which are filled with white paint.

Painted and Intrusive Pottery

Encinas Red-on-brown (Sayles 1945: 43). This is a diagnostic decorated type during the Nantack Phase and comprises 33.3% of all painted and intrusive sherds.

Arthur H. Rohn, Jr., graduate student in the Department of Anthropology, University of Arizona, made a microscopic examination of 95 Encinas Red-on-brown sherds from Nantack Village. He also examined 50 sherds of this type from San Simon Village. His findings show that macroscopically there is no difference in Encinas Red-on-brown from either site. However, 72% of the sherds from Nantack Village contain leucite tuff, a commonly occurring material in the Point of Pines region. This is substantial proof that at least some Encinas Red-on-brown is indigenous at Nantack Village and consequently expands the area of distribution of this type. The place of origin of Encinas Red-on-brown is not clear, but the relative amount of material from Nantack Village favors the Point of Pines rather than the San Simon region as the locality of manufacture.

There is a late variant of Encinas Red-on-brown at Point of Pines which is found in the Reserve and Tularosa phases and which is represented by two or three sherds from Pithouse 10. This late variety frequently has a thin creamy slip which is sometimes scored. The paint is the color of dried blood and there is no polishing over the decoration. A sherd which is photographically similar to this late variety is pictured by Sayles (1945, Pl. 26, *f*).

New Type: Nantack Red-on-Brown

During excavation the sherds of this type were considered to be a broad-line variety of Encinas Red-on-brown. Laboratory reanalysis and comparison with material from San Simon Village showed this assumption to be false. Differences between Encinas Red-on-brown and Nantack Red-on-brown are readily seen in Figure 25.

Five of the 75 sherds of Nantack Red-on-brown were examined microscopically. The paste is the same as that described for Pine Flat Neck Corrugated. Since the color of the red design does not differ, macroscopically, from redwares found

Fig. 25. Red-on-brown sherds. *a-d*, Nantack Red-on-brown; *e*, *f*, Encinas Red-on-brown. *b*, 5.7 cm. long.

at Nantack Village it is postulated that Nantack Red-on-brown is a local combination of Encinas Red-on-brown and San Francisco-Reserve reds.

Designs are predominantly triangles pendant from the rim. Only bowl forms are known.

Wheat (1954: 89) reports the presence of a similar type from Crooked Ridge Village. The time discrepancy amounts to about 300 years when comparing the two sites: Crooked Ridge Village, pre-600(?), and Nantack Village, post-900.

Technologically and typologically Nantack Red-on-brown resembles Cascabel Red-on-brown (Tuthill 1947: 50) with one exception. Cascabel Red-on-brown always has a red-slipped exterior and Nantack Red-on-brown has an unslipped exterior.

Gladwin (1948: 164) speaks of a short-lived, broad-line red-on-brown stage between the earliest Mogollon polished redware and the later, fine-line red-on-browns. He equates this broad-line red-on-brown period with Estrella Red-on-gray and Dos Cabezas Red-on-brown (1948: 218). I think broad-line red-on-browns were made from about A.D. 600 (Dos Cabezas Red-on-brown, Circle Prairie Phase at Crooked Ridge Village) until A.D. 1000, the Encinas, Cascabel and Nantack red-on-brown period, with no major typological or technological innovations. During the last half of this period the broad-line red-on-browns admittedly became less common, but broad-line red-on-browns are not in themselves indicators of early Mogollon horizons.

Hohokam Intrusives

Of all intrusive sherds 20.9% are Hohokam in origin.

Santa Cruz Red-on-buff (Gladwin and others 1937: 179–85). The four sherds are from house fill.

Sacaton Red-on-buff (Gladwin and others 1937: 171–8). The 50 sherds indicate trade with the Gila-Salt Basin.

Sacaton Red-on-buff, Safford Variety. The 271 sherds recognized as the Safford region variant of Sacaton Red-on-buff comprise 10.5% of all intrusives. This is a diagnostic trade type during the Nantack Phase.

Buff Ware, Gila Basin and *Buff Ware, Safford Region.* The Buff Ware classification designates those Hohokam sherds without painted decoration or decoration too small to be classified as to type. The two categories are determined by paste characteristics and indicate trade with these two regions of the Hohokam area.

Gila Plain (Gladwin and others 1937: 205–11). The even distribution of the 87 sherds throughout the pithouse units indicates Hohokam trade affiliations for the whole time span of the Nantack Phase.

Mimbres Intrusives

Of all intrusive sherds 27% are from the Mimbres region.

Mangas Black-on-white (Haury 1936a: 22; previously called Mimbres Bold Face Black-on-white by Cosgrove 1932: 76). Encinas Red-on-brown is the only decorated type which is more abundant than Mangas Black-on-white. It is a diagnostic trade type during the Nantack Phase. A Mangas Black-on-white jar was found on the floor of Pithouse 8 (Fig. 26).

Mimbres Black-on-white (Cosgrove 1932: 72–5). This type is only one-fifth as abundant as Mangas Black-on-white. Mimbres Black-on-white generally occurs higher in the fill of pithouse excavations than Mangas Black-on-white, except in Pithouse 10 and the trash mound over Pithouse 9.

Mimbres White Ware. Seventy sherds have the paste of pottery made in the Mimbres region but either contain no painted decoration or the design is too small to be accurately classified as either Mangas Black-on-white or Mimbres Black-on-white.

Other Intrusives

Showlow Black-on-red (Colton and Hargrave 1937: 78). The three sherds, all from the Great Kiva fill, are indigenous in the region of Chambers, Arizona, north of the White Mountains.

Fig. 26. Jar of Mangas Black-on-white. Maximum height, 32.5 cm.

Puerco Black-on-red (Colton and Hargrave 1937: 120). Three sherds of this type indicate late Nantack trade with the Rio Puerco region. They are associated with Pithouse 10, the latest semi-subterranean unit, and the trash mound over Pithouse 9.

Wingate Black-on-red (Colton and Hargrave 1937: 118). The 16 sherds are associated with house fill, except in the cases of Pithouse 10 and the trash mound over Pithouse 9. They, again, show the relative lateness of these features. A Wingate Black-on-red jar was found in the floor fill of Pithouse 3 (Fig. 27).

Within the category of Wingate Black-on-red are sherds of North Plains Black-on-red (Olson and Wasley 1956: 303). This type is contemporaneous with Wingate Black-on-red and is highly polished with fine-line, iron paint decorations.

Unknown Black-on-red. Four of the 11 untypable black-on-red sherds lack diagnostic features. The remaining seven sherds are an unnamed, highly polished, carbon paint type that E. B. Danson believes were made in the White Mountains. Three of these seven sherds have a narrow-line decoration and four have a broad-line decoration.

Tularosa White-on-red (Wendorf 1950: 122). The one sherd from the fill of Pithouse 4 probably belongs to the overlying surface rooms of Ruin B.

Deadmans Black-on-gray (Colton and Hargrave 1937: 253). The two sherds of this Cohonina type are both from house fill.

Unknown Gray Ware. These 10 sherds lack decoration but indicate trade connections with the Anasazi area.

Kiatuthlanna Black-on-white (Hawley 1936: 27). Contact with the Cibola region is indicated by these seven sherds.

Corduroy Black-on-white. The one sherd is from the fill of a main support posthole in the Great Kiva. This type is indigenous to the Forestdale Valley during the 800-900 period and will be described in Haury's forthcoming report on the Forestdale Valley.

Red Mesa Black-on-white (Gladwin 1945: 56–7). Contact with the Cibola Branch is indicated by 37 sherds. Their association with floor

FIG. 27. Jar of Wingate Black-on-red. Maximum diameter at handles 15.2 cm.

fill makes their use in interpretation more valid than those types occurring only in pithouse fill.

Holbrook Black-on-white (Colton 1955b). Three sherds, from the house fill of Pithouse 6, indicated trade with the Little Colorado River valley.

Puerco Black-on-white (Hawley 1936: 34). Again, contact with the Cibola region is indicated by the presence of nine sherds of this type. Only in the Great Kiva are Puerco Black-on-white sherds found below house fill levels.

Snowflake Black-on-white. The 47 sherds have the paste characteristics of Snowflake Black-on-white from the Forestdale Valley. This type will be described in Haury's forthcoming report on the Forestdale Valley. Only three sherds are from below house fill levels.

Pueblo II Glaze Black-on-white. Eight sherds of this unnamed and undescribed type were identified from the Forestdale Valley study collections at the Arizona State Museum.

Whipple Black-on-white (Colton 1941: 60). The one sherd is from the trash mound forming the house fill of Pithouse 9.

Reserve Black-on-white (Martin and Rinaldo 1950b: 502-19). The relative abundance of this post-Nantack type is misleading. The 139 sherds are consistently associated with the house fill of pithouse units and indicate post-Nantack Phase occupation of the pithouse depressions. Within the classification of Reserve Black-on-white is a subtype called Early Reserve by Danson (1957: 92). Early Reserve has characteristics of Red Mesa and Puerco Black-on-whites and Mimbres types.

Tularosa Black-on-white (Rinaldo and Bluhm 1956: 177–85). The three sherds are from house fill of pithouses and are indicative of the post-Nantack Phase occupation.

Pinedale Black-on-white (Colton and Hargrave 1937: 241). The one sherd, from the house fill of Pithouse 4, is probably associated with the overlying surface rooms of Ruin B.

Unknown Northern Black-on-whites. These 66 sherds of northern origin lack diagnostic decorative features which can be used for typing.

Northern White Wares. None of these 37 Anasazi sherds have any painted decoration.

Little Colorado Corrugated (Colton 1955b). The two sherds are from the Great Kiva.

St. Johns Polychrome (Colton and Hargrave 1937: 104). Both sherds, from the house fill of Pithouses 3 and 4, are associated with the post-Nantack Phase occupation.

Maverick Mountain Polychrome (Referred to as Unnamed Polychrome by Wendorf 1950: 124–5). One sherd of this local copy of Kiet Siel Polychrome is from the fill of the Great Kiva.

Whole Vessels

The 20 whole or restorable vessels, excepting miniatures, consist of the following types:

Alma Smudged bowls	2
Alma Plain jars (Fig. 19 *a, d*)	3
Alma Plain pitcher (Fig. 19 *b*)	1
Alma Plain dish (Fig. 19 *c*)	1
San Francisco Red jar (Fig. 20 *a*)	1
Reserve Red bowl (Fig. 20 *b*)	1
Three Circle Neck Corrugated jars (Fig. 21)	6
Pine Flat Neck Corrugated jars (Figs. 22 *b-d*, 23)	3
Mangas Black-on-white jar (Fig. 26)	1
Wingate Black-on-red jar (Fig. 27)	1
Total	20

Miniature Vessels

Six pottery vessels with all dimensions less than 10.0 cm. are classified as miniatures. Four of the vessels could be used as utensils and two, both hand-modeled jars, are not utilitarian.

Description	Provenience	Illustration
Redware pitcher	Burial 2	Fig. 28 *e*
Plainware seed jar	Burial 2	Fig. 28 *a*
Plainware jar	Burial 2	Fig. 28 *d*
Three Circle Neck Corrugated pitcher	Burial 2	Fig. 28 *b*
Plainware jar	Great Kiva Fill	
Plainware smudged bowl	Pithouse 10, Floor	

One of the two ladles is plain, with solid handle (Fig. 28 *c*). Dimensions: inside diameter of bowl, 3.1 by 4.0 cm.; depth of bowl, 1.6 cm.; length of handle, 4.3 cm. The other ladle is

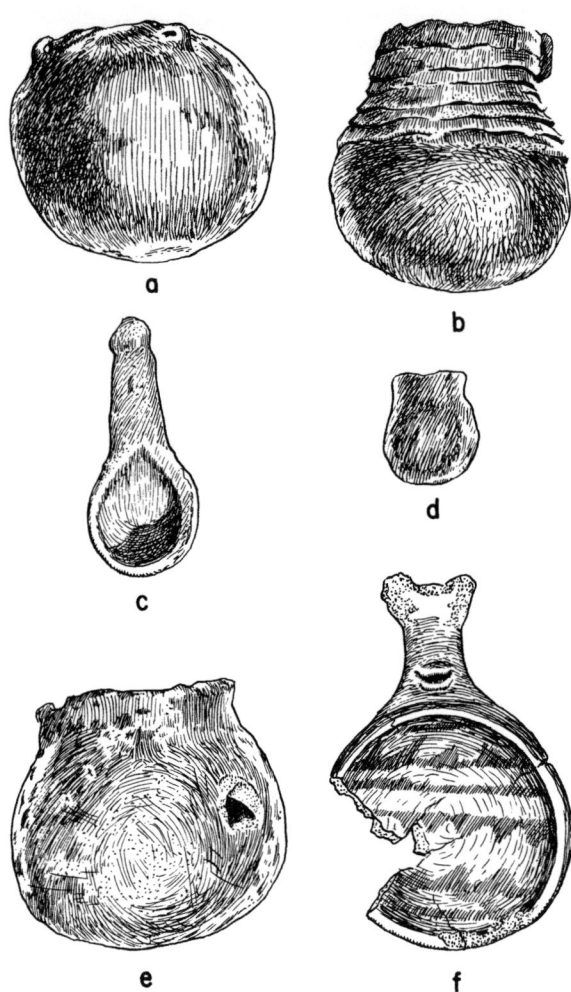

Fig. 28. Miniature vessels. *a*, plainware seed jar; *b*, Three Circle Neck Corrugated pitcher; *c*, plainware ladle; *d*, plainware jar; *e*, redware pitcher; *f*, Encinas Red-on-brown ladle. Length of *c*, 8.3 cm.

Encinas Red-on-brown with effigy handle which resembles fox's head (Fig. 28 f). Dimensions: inside diameter of bowl, 7.0 cm.; depth of bowl, 3.3 cm.; length of handle, 4.4 cm. Both miniature ladles are associated with Burial 2.

MISCELLANEOUS POTTERY OBJECTS

Figurines. Only caudal and body portions of the three hand-modeled, quadruped figurines are represented.

Provenience: House fill, Pithouse 9 (1); Great Kiva (1); Test 17 (1).

Sherd discs, Perforate (Fig. 29 a-f, h). All 55 specimens have biconical perforations through the general center; the majority have ground edges but 11 of the saved specimens are not ground. A few specimens are oblong to square and do not fit the classification of "spindle whorls."

Materials: Redware bowls (20), Plainware jars (10), Redware jars (8), Plainware bowls (6), Mangas Black-on-white (6), Mimbres White Ware (2), Wingate Black-on-red (1), Gila Plain (1), Reserve Indented Corrugated (1).

Provenience: Floor, Pithouses 1 (1), 6 (1); Floor fill, Pithouses 1 (7), 4 (1), 5 (1), Great Kiva (1); House fill, Pithouses 1 (5), 3 (1), 4 (3), 5 (2), 6 (4), 8 (4), 9 (6), 10 (2), Great Kiva (11); Posthole fill, Great Kiva (2); Pit fill, Pithouse 8 (1); Surface (2).

Sherd Discs, Imperforate (Fig. 29 g, i-l). The majority of the 34 imperforate sherd discs have ground edges; six have conical holes started from one side; one has conical holes started from both.

Materials: Plainware jars (16), Redware jars (6), Plainware bowls (5), Redware bowls (2), Mangas Black-on-white (1), Puerco Black-on-white (1), Encinas Red-on-brown (1), Nantack Red-on-brown (1), Unknown Black-on-white (1).

Provenience: Floor, Pithouse 5 (1); Floor fill, Pithouse 10 (2); House fill, Pithouses 1 (2), 3 (3), 4 (2), 5 (3), 6 (2), 8 (2), 9 (8), Great Kiva (3); Posthole fill, Great Kiva (3); Floor pit fill, Great Kiva (1); Test 16 (1); Surface (1).

Worked Sherds, Fragments. Twelve shaped sherds too incomplete to determine if they are perforated or unperforated are classified as fragments.

Materials: Plainware jars (3), Plainware bowls (2), Redware bowls (2), Encinas Red-on-brown (2), Mangas Black-on-white (2), Redware jars (1).

Provenience: Floor fill, Pithouse 1 (1), House fill, Pithouses 6 (2), 8 (1), 9 (2), Great Kiva (3); Posthole fill, Great Kiva (2); Test 16 (1).

Sherd Scrapers. The 15 sherd scrapers have a well-ground, beveled working edge, or edges.

Materials: Redware bowls (5), Plainware jars (3), Mangas Black-on-white (3), Plainware bowls (2), Encinas Red-on-brown (1), Nantack Red-on-brown (1).

Provenience: Floor fill, Pithouses 5 (1), 9 (1), 10 (3), Great Kiva (1); House fill, Pithouses 1 (1), 9 (2), Great Kiva (3); Posthole fill, Great Kiva (1); Tests 16 (1), 18 (1).

Incised Sherd (Fig. 30 b). Redware bowl sherd; rubbed on three edges and broken on bot-

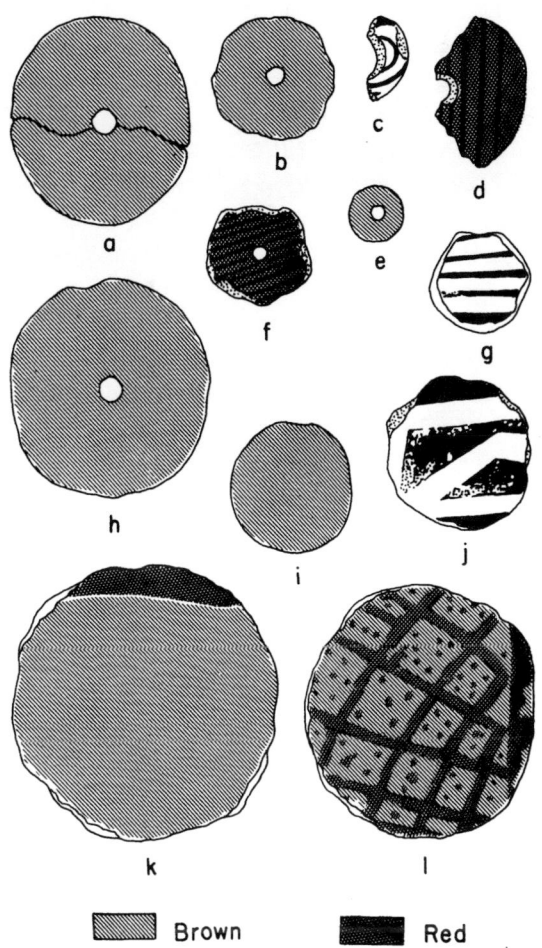

FIG. 29. Sherd discs. *a-f, h,* perforated sherd discs; *g, i-l,* unperforated sherd discs. Diameter of *k,* 8.2 cm.

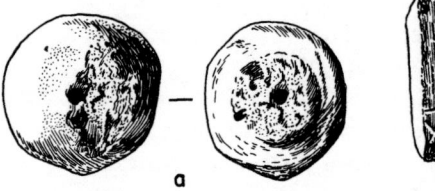

Fig. 30. Fragment of unidentified clay object and incised sherd. *a*, two faces of unidentified clay object; *b*, incised sherd. Width of *b*, 23 mm.

tom; a face scratched on the concave surface has two roundish eyes and teeth formed by crosshatching. Dimensions: length, 22 mm.; width, 23 mm.; thickness, 5 mm.

Provenience: Floor fill, Great Kiva.

Ceramic Tube Fragment. Designated on basis of comparison with two complete specimens from Ruin C, Room 2 (Fig. 47).

Provenience: Kiva fill, Great Kiva.

Tail of Duck Effigy(?). Hand-modeled, plainware object with shape of tail for duck effigy vessel; upper surface has ten parallel incised lines.

Provenience: House fill, Pithouse 5.

Fragment of Unidentified Clay Object (Fig. 30 *a*). Hand-modeled, roughly spherical, plainware; cylindrical perforation; has broken from rest of object at constriction on the under side. Dimensions: diameter, 25 mm.; thickness, 21 mm.; diameter of perforation, 2 mm.

Provenience: Floor fill, Pithouse 10.

DISCUSSION

Ceramically, Pithouses 1, 5 and 8 and the Great Kiva are considered the type units for the Nantack Phase. Pithouses 3 and 6 are also Nantack Phase but Pithouse 6 gives the impression of being early and Pithouse 3 of being late in the phase. Encinas Red-on-brown and Sacaton Red-on-buff are not present in Pithouse 3. Pithouse 2 does not contain enough ceramic material to place it in the Nantack Phase. Pithouse 4 is a Nantack Phase unit and the ceramic mixture is attributed to the overlying surface rooms of Ruin B. Pithouse 9 has all the types designated as dianostic for the Nantack Phase but on the basis of over-all types represented and percentages this unit resembles Pithouse 10. The higher percentage of "later" black-on-red and black-on-white types from Pithouse 10 indicates that it is younger than all(?) of the other semi-subterranean units at Nantack Village.

TRASH MOUND

Trash mounds are not associated with pre-1000 Mogollon sites; however, one overlies Pithouse 9. Pithouse 10, a large semi-subterranean structure, is located 20 to 25 meters upslope and to the west of Pithouse 9 and the trenched trash mound. The ceramic complex of Pithouse 10 indicates that it is younger than the other pithouses at Nantack Village. It is postulated that the trash mound superimposed over Pithouse 9 is the result of the construction of Pithouse 10. Indications are that the trash and humus from the excavation of Pithouse 10 were collected and dumped in a single, relatively small area to form the trash mound. The general homogeneity of the trash mound points to its deposition in a short time. While digging the trash mound trench there was a feeling of reverse stratigraphy, but this is not apparent from the sherd tabulations.

The ceramic-stratigraphic evidence and the positional conditions suggest strongly that the trash mound over Pithouse 9 is the result of the dumping of debris from the construction of Pithouse 10. If this hypothesis is not correct then the occurrence of the trash mound is unique for Mogollon sites of this period and its presence must be attributed to Hohokam or Anasazi influence.

PLAINWARE

The plainware from Nantack Village consists of Alma Plain and the varieties of the Alma Series. They are by far the most abundant types recovered and are made with local paste.

REDWARE

Both San Francisco Red and Reserve Red, Point of Pines varieties are recognized from the pithouses. Their occurrence in the same units indicates their contemporaneity during the 900-1000 time period. The several varieties of San Francisco Red denote an elaboration or experimentation with redware pottery during the Nantack Phase.

TEXTURED POTTERY

Neck corrugation is the typical texturing technique during the Nantack Phase. Reserve Indented Corrugated also is considered as a diagnostic pottery type. All-over corrugated pottery is not a characteristic of the 900–1000 period in the Reserve and Mimbres regions. However, elaboration of textured pottery is a characteristic of post-Nantack Phase periods in the Point of Pines region (Breternitz, Gifford and Olson 1957; Wendorf 1950: 36–41). This later proliferation of surface manipulated types is forecast by the variety of textured pottery made during the Nantack Phase. The occurrence of certain methods of texturing during the Nantack Phase in the Point of Pines region negates the value of comparing textured pottery in other regions, or branches, and then attempting to apply "pottery dates" of utility types through space.

Alternative proposals to the proposition that such texturing techniques as over-all corrugation are earlier in the Black River Branch include: (1) The assignment of the Nantack Phase to the 900–1000 period is erroneous and should be extended possibly 50 years or, (2) there is a contamination due to the presence of post-Nantack Phase dwellings at the site.

PAINTED AND INTRUSIVE POTTERY

The ceramic complex at Nantack Village indicates that the Nantack Phase is contemporary with the Three Circle Phase in the Mimbres and Reserve branches, and to a lesser extent with the Cerros and Encinas phases in the San Simon Branch.

Three Circle Phase houses at the SU site have the same ceramic complex, with two exceptions. There is no Three Circle Red-on-white from Nantack Village and no Reserve Indented Corrugated from the SU site (Martin and Rinaldo 1947: 369). The lack of Three Circle Red-on-white at Nantack Village is notable. Perhaps a half dozen sherds of Mangas Black-on-white verge on being Three Circle Red-on-white. This absence of a type considered typical of the 900–1000 period in the Mimbres region can be explained in at least two ways. First, the pithouse occupation of Nantack Village occurred subsequent to the time that Three Circle Red-on-white was made, or secondly, there could have been a local preference for Mangas Black-on-white. Three Circle Red-on-white has a short history and this should be taken into consideration. Also, Cerros Red-on-white, the San Simon Branch equivalent of Three Circle Red-on-white, is not found at Nantack Village.

The presence of Reserve Black-on-white in the fill of pithouses assigned to the 900–1000 period is not unique. At Starkweather Ruin (Nesbitt 1938: 81) and Harris Village (Haury 1936b: 66) a similar situation occurred.

Similarities between Nantack, Dos Cabezas and Cascabel red-on-browns have been mentioned. Red-on-brown bowls with broad-line designs and polishing over the decoration, apparently were made by the Mogollon during a 400-year period beginning about A.D. 600. They are, relatively, less frequent during the last 200 years of the period but do continue as minor types until around A.D. 1000.

At least some of the Encinas Red-on-brown from Nantack Village is idigenous. The consistency of the type indicates a close contact between the Black River and San Simon branches during the Nantack Phase.

All regions surrounding Point of Pines contribute to the inventory of intrusive pottery types except the west. Encinas Red-on-brown(?), the Sacaton and Safford varieties of Sacaton Red-on-buff, Mangas Black-on-white, and numerous "Northern" black-on-whites are considered to be the diagnostic trade types during the Nantack Phase.

When taking into consideration the discrepancies inherent with a difference in locality, the ceramic complex at Nantack Village closely resembles the original definition of the Three Circle Phase, A.D. 900–1000 (Haury 1936a: 42).

MISCELLANEOUS POTTERY OBJECTS

Sherd discs, both perforated and unperforated, are type artifacts for the Nantack Phase. Due to the range in size, shape, degree of alteration, and

TABLE 2. PLAIN, RED AND TEXTURED SHERDS FROM PITHOUSES, GREAT KIVA, AND BURIALS

Pottery Types	1 House Fill	1 Storage Fill	2 Fill	3 Fill	4 House Fill	4 Floor	5 House Fill	5 Floor Fill	6 House Fill	6 Floor Fill	7 House Fill	7 Floor Fill	8 House Fill	8 Floor Fill	9 Fill	10 House Fill	10 Floor Fill	Great Kiva Fill	Great Kiva Floor Fill	Burials 1	Burials 2	Burials 3	Burials 4
Alma Plain	3587	37	83	2205	344	80	1984	73	2525	262	710	45	812	397	4588	1524	851	8830	2500	81	6	40	12
Alma Smudged	230		2	60	38	16	68	38	95	9	42	7	23	19	248	80	38	349	179	4	5	1	
Alma Polished	48	1		76			29	57	70	6	12	1	14	17	97	19	17	174	65			3	
Alma Rough								1	8			1	12		17				7				
Alma Scored	22		1	11			70	71		1	2		13	7	31	23	18	15	48			1	
Alma Incised	3			1			1		4						2	2		13	1				
Alma Punched	16						1	1	1						3	7	2	11	6	1			
Alma Grooved							1		1						3								
Redware Jars	547	4	3	203	27	8	279	85	210	19	71	2	56	32	663	213	77	1086	420	17	3	6	
Redware Bowls	340	3	12	219	22	8	217	83	276	21	95	2	73	45	555	148	91	881	318	4		11	9
Redware Smudged				32	18	4	10	6	13	3	4		5	6	42	11	10	64	17	7		1	
San Francisco Red, Coiled Exterior				14			6	3	2				1	3	10	5		3	8				
San Francisco Red, Punched Exterior					1		1												1				
Alma Neck Banded							13	4	10		1		4	4				15	15				
Three Circle Neck Corrugated	80	1	2	1				4	52	4			24	14	175	44	22	159	54			2	1
Pine Flat Neck Corrugated	472	6	6	61			191	85	98	12	28	3	27	10	330	106	46	932	225	7	2	4	1
Obliterated Neck Corrugated	55		6	39			16	13	41	7				12	29	8	11	3	39				
Reserve Incised Corrugated	6			6			5	3	4		3		5	2	46	18	5	100	19				
Reserve Punched Corrugated									1					2		4	1	17	4				
Reserve Plain Corrugated	9		2	41	47	5	27	6	13	1	7				3	38	18	115	12	4			
Reserve Indented Corrugated	14		6	153	103	15	87	14	31		36		6	1	101	48	25	129	38	11			
Red Slipped Corrugated				11			9	1							8	3	1	2	1				
Tularosa Patterned Corrugated			4	34	11		7		1				2		16	5	1	19	2				
Prieto Indented Corrugated							1		1		1			1		1	1		2				
Point of Pines Obliterated Corrugated				36	8		26				1		15			9	10	115	1	4			
Point of Pines Punctate							2								1	2		1					
Reserve Fillet Rim															1								
Tularosa Fillet Rim					11	1	5				1				1	1	1	5					
McDonald Painted Corrugated				8	3											1							
McDonald Patterned Corrugated				6	5	2	14	2								3	1						
McDonald Grooved Corrugated				2	1													3	3				
Total	5430	52	121	3219	639	139	3070	1151	3457	345	1014	61	1092	572	6970	2323	1246	13041	3985	140	16	70	23

36

Table 3. Painted and Intrusive Sherds From Pithouses, Great Kiva, and Burials

Pottery Types	1 House Fill	1 Storage Pit Fill	2 Fill	3 Fill	4 House Fill	4 Floor Fill	5 House Fill	5 Floor Fill	6 House Fill	6 Floor Fill	7 House Fill	7 Floor Fill	8 House Fill	8 Floor Fill	9 Fill	10 House Fill	10 Floor Fill	Kiva Fill	Floor Fill	B1	B2	B3	B4
Encinas Red-on-brown	131			18			59	12	44	1	21		10	5	116	18	10	325	85	4			4
Nantack Red-on-brown	1	2	1				1	2	10				1		12	1	2	34	11				
Santa Cruz Red-on-buff															2	1	1						
Sacaton Red-on-buff												1		1	26	6	1	7	3				
Sacaton Red-on-buff, Safford Variety	16						33	13	5		7				23	7	8	131	28	1	1		
Buff Ware, Gila Basin	4						1	1	3		4		1		*23	4		4	7				
Buff Ware, Safford Region							25	12	8	2				3		5	2	14	8				
Gila Plain	17			2			3	1	1		5		1		23	2		15	9				
Showlow Black-on-red																		3					
Puerco Black-on-red	1														1	2	1	2	1				
Wingate Black-on-red									1						5	4		4	1			1	
Unknown Black-on-red				1										1	1	4							
Tularosa White-on-red					1	1																	
Mangas Black-on-white	35			17			24	17	40	3	12		14	9	86	14	14	197	48				
Mimbres Black-on-white	4						20		17		1		3		15	1	2	30	7				
Mimbres White Ware	4			6			8	2	4		1	1	1	1	19	1		9	13				
Deadmans Black-on-gray	1																						
Gray Wares													4		2	1	2		1				
Kiatuthlanna Black-on-white	1		1	2					1		1						1		1				
Corduroy Black-on-white																			1				
Red Mesa Black-on-white	8			1			3	2								2		19	2				
Holbrook Black-on-white									3														
Puerco Black-on-white							1								1			3	4				
Snowflake Black-on-white							3				2				19	2	1	20					
PII Glaze Black-on-white															2	2		2	2				
Whipple Black-on-white															1								
Reserve Black-on-white	6			2	5		9	4	3		3				22	16	14	51	9				
Tularosa Black-on-white				1							1				1								
Pinedale Black-on-white					1																		1
Unknown Northern Black-on-white	13		2				6		8	1	3		2	1	7	4	1	10	5				
Northern White Wares															16			15	6				
Little Colorado Corrugated																		1	1				
Maverick Mountain Polychrome																		1					
St. Johns Polychrome					1																		
Total	242	2	4	52	8	1	196	66	154	9	62	1	37	20	425	95	60	897	252	5	1	2	1

*Gila Basin Buff Ware and Safford Region Buff Ware not separated

types of pottery used no conjectures as to their use are advanced. It is obvious, however, that the majority are not spindle whorls.

Sherd scrapers have a beveled working edge, which could be employed efficiently for thinning the vessel walls of pottery made by the coil and scrape method.

The distribution of miscellaneous clay artifacts given by Wheat (1955: 107) for Mogollon 4 in the Black River Branch may be amended. Perforated discs are abundant; sherd discs are common; animal figurines and sherd scrapers are present. Miniature vessels and ladles probably occur but due to the association of these objects with a child's skeleton, Burial 2, their assignment to the Nantack Phase is tenuous. Pottery pipes, cornucopias, human figurines, clay pot covers, sherd scoops, sherd pendants and sherd sieves are not included in the inventory of miscellaneous ceramic objects from the Nantack Phase occupation of Nantack Village.

STONE ARTIFACTS

The descriptions of non-ceramic artifacts are given in expanded outline. Measurements for each artifact are not given unless it is a necessary part of the description. A tabulation of dimensions for the artifact groupings is on file at the Library, University of Arizona (Breternitz 1956).

For the descriptions of stone artifacts over-all sizes are named in reference to the geological size scale. This scale is: pebble, 2 mm. to 64 mm.; cobble, 65 mm. to 256 mm.; boulder, greater than 256 mm. in diameter.

Artifacts found on the floor are also listed with the architectural description of each pithouse.

Artifacts are grouped according to technique of manufacture and as they are believed to have been used.

Ground Stone

Stone tools produced by pecking, grinding, drilling or polishing, those resulting from use, and those resulting from a combination of techniques are termed *ground stone tools*. They are classified as follows:

	Individual Types	Total
Metates		15
Type 1, flat boulder	1	
Type 2, full basin	5	
Type 3a, closed-end trough, or "scoop"	8	
Type 3b, "Utah" type	1	
Grinding slabs		6
Type 1a, uniface, unshaped	2	
Type 1b, uniface, shaped	1	
Type 2, biface, shaped	3	
Manos		55
Type 1a, uniface, round to oval	21	
Type 1b, uniface, rectangular	19	
Type 1c, uniface, ridged	1	
Type 2a, biface, round to oval	10	
Type 2b, biface, rectangular	4	
Handstones		25
Type 1, uniface	6	
Type 2, biface	19	
Pestles		2
Stone bowls		6
Type 1a, circular tuff bowls	2	
Type 1b, hemispherical tuff bowls	2	
Type 2, discoidal quartzite bowl	1	
Type 3, hemispherical quartzite bowl, painted	1	
Stone dish		1
Pitted tuff discoids		2
Stone ring		1
Palettes		5
Type 1, Hohokam	3	
Type 2, Mogollon	2	
Effigies		2
Type 1, Anthropomorphic(?)	1	
Type 2, Quadrupedal	1	
Problematical stone		1
Polishing stones		13
Type 1, pebble	11	
Type 2, flat stone	2	
Abrading stones		13
Type 1, uniface	6	
Type 2, biface	7	
Grooved abrading stone		1
Shaped stones		2
Hammerstones		67
Type 1, spherical to angular	67	
Grooved mauls		3

Grooved tuff cobble	1
Three-quarter grooved axes	2
Ornaments	10
Disc beads	9
Hematite disc	1
Total	234

METATES

Type 1 (Fig. 31 *a*). One specimen; made from unshaped boulder; grinding surface flat; grinding motion could be longitudinal or lateral.

Material: Fine-grained basalt (1).
Provenience: Floor, Pithouse 5 (1).

Type 2 (Fig. 31 *b*). Five specimens; made from boulders, usually unshaped; grinding surface shallow to deep, oval, closed basin; grinding motion essentially longitudinal but semi-rotary. Type 1a and 2a manos and Type 1 and 2 handstones could be used with Type 2 metates. Two are bifacial; one worn out.

Material: Fine-grained basalt (3), vesicular basalt (1), unknown (1).
Provenience: Floor, Pithouses 1 (1), 7 (1); Floor pits, Great Kiva (2); Posthole fill, Great Kiva (1).

Type 3a (Fig. 31 *c*). Eight specimens; trough metate closed at one end; made from selected boulders, usually unshaped. One specimen biface; one worn out; one shattered and possibly full-trough metate. Grinding motion longitudinal, with mano filling width of trough. Type 1b and 2b manos and some handstones are suitable for use in Type 3a metates.

Material: Fine-grained basalt (6), vesicular basalt (1), porphyritic basalt (1).
Provenience: Floor, Pithouses 3 (1), 4 (1), 6 (1), 8 (1), 10 (1); House fill, Pithouses 5 (1), 6 (1); Area northwest of Pithouse 10 (1).

Type 3b (Fig. 31 *d*). One specimen; "Utah" type; similar to Type 3a but has a small shelf or basin at rear end, commonly thought to be a mano "rest."

Material: Fine-grained basalt (1).
Provenience: Floor, Pithouse 6 (1).

GRINDING SLABS

Type 1a. Two specimens; uniface; unshaped basalt slabs; grinding surface flat except one on larger specimen which is slightly basin; grinding surface extends to edge of slab in one specimen.

Material: Fine-grained basalt (1), porphyritic basalt (1).
Provenience: Floor, Pithouse 3 (1); House fill, Pithouse 3 (1).

Type 1b (Fig. 32 *a*). One specimen; uniface; over-all shape same as Type 1a mano but with

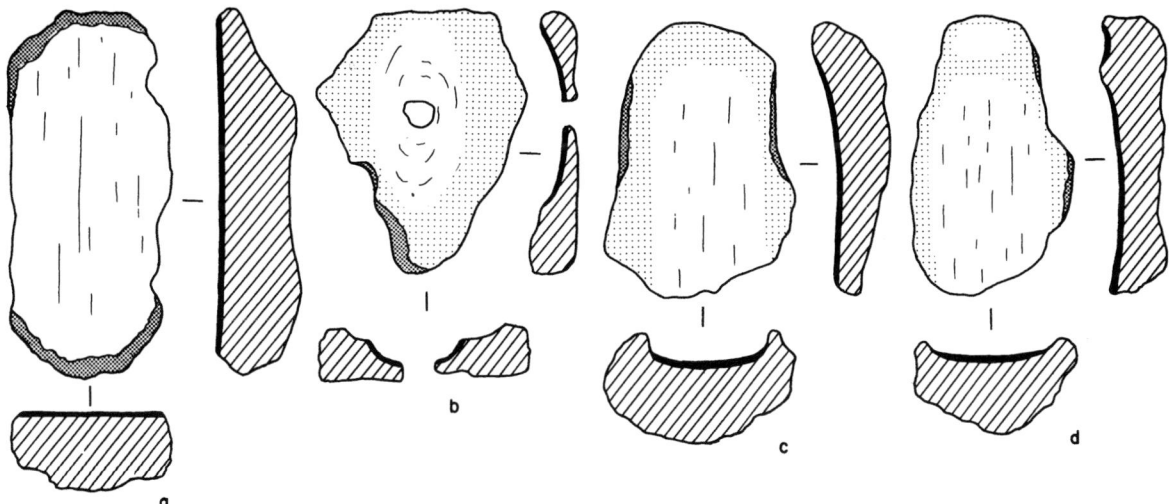

FIG. 31. Metates. *a*, flat, boulder; *b*, full basin; *c*, closed-end trough; *d*, "Utah." Heavy lines in cross-sections indicate grinding surfaces. Length of *d*, 43.5 cm.

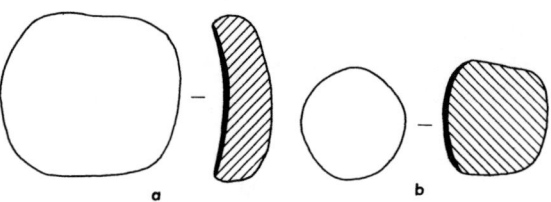

Fig. 32. Grinding slab and pestle. *a*, grinding slab; *b*, pestle. Heavy lines in cross-sections indicate grinding surfaces. Length of *a*, 12.7 cm.

shallow grinding basin; grinding basin slightly concave in both axes; edges and opposite side shaped.

Material: Fine-grained basalt (1).
Provenience: Fill, Storage pit, Pithouse 1 (1).

Type 2. Three specimens; biface; concave grinding surface; opposite grinding surface slightly to moderately convex like Type 1a and 2a manos. Two specimens have traces of red pigment on concave grinding surface; one has pigment on convex grinding surface. These grinding slabs are like Type 1b grinding slabs but in addition are reused manos.

Material: Vesicular basalt (2), fine-grained basalt (1).
Provenience: Floor, Pithouses 5 (1), 8 (1); House fill, Pithouse 8 (1).

Manos and Handstones

The term *mano* is limited here to the generally large, relatively thin, elongated tool presumably used in trough metates for grinding corn. The generally small, relatively thick and broad forms presumably used for other grinding purposes are here termed *handstones*. Within these two broad classes are variations in number of grinding surfaces and over-all shape. These groups and their subtypes are classified as follows:

Manos

Type 1a (Fig. 33 *a*). Twenty-one specimens; uniface; round to ovoid, grading imperceptibly into subrectangular; usually shaped around edges by pecking; grinding surfaces slightly to moderately convex on longitudinal axis and less convex on transverse axis; two worn out specimens have lenticular sections. These manos could be used in Type 3a and 3b metates; some small ones could be used in Type 2 metates.

Material: Vesicular basalt (8), sandstone (6), fine-grained basalt (5), quartzite (1), tuff (1).
Provenience: Floor, Pithouses 1 (2), 3 (1), 6 (3), 8 (4), Great Kiva (1); Floor fill, Pithouse 1 (1); House fill, Pithouses 5 (1), 6 (1), 8 (1), 9 (1), 10 (1); Posthole fill, Pithouse 3 (1); Storage pit, Pithouse 1 (1); Area northwest of Pithouse 10 (1); Test pit 17 (1).

Type 1b (Fig. 33 *e*). Nineteen specimens; uniface, rectangular; longitudinal axis at least one-third again as long as the width, usually longer; edges often shaped by pecking; grinding surface moderately convex on longitudinal axis and flat to slightly convex on transverse axis; opposite surface often shaped. Four specimens have pecked finger grooves for gripping. These could be used in wide troughed Type 3a and 3b metates.

Material: Vesicular basalt (9), fine-grained basalt (5), quartzite (4), porphyritic basalt (1).
Provenience: Floor, Pithouses 1 (3), 3 (1), 6 (3), 8 (1), 10 (1); Posthole, Pithouse 1 (1); Floor pits, Pithouse 5 (2); House fill, Pithouses 2 (1), 3 (1), 6 (1), 8 (1), Great Kiva (3).

Type 1c (Fig. 33 *d*). One specimen; uniface; rectangular edges shaped by pecking; two-faceted grinding surface has marked longitudinal ridge.

Material: Tuff (1).
Provenience: House fill, Pithouse 6 (1).

Type 2a (Fig. 33 *b*). Ten specimens; biface; round to oval, grading imperceptibly into subrectangular; minority are shaped around edges by pecking; grinding surfaces slightly convex on both axes. One specimen has red pigment stain on grinding surface; two have wedge-shaped sections. Grinding striations indicate use in Type 3a and 3b metates.

Material: Fine-grained basalt (6), vesicular basalt (4).
Provience: Floor, Pithouses 6 (3), 8 (1), 10 (1); House fill, Pithouses 4 (1), 6 (2), 8 (2).

Type 2b. Four specimens; biface; rectangular, with longitudinal axis at least one-third again as long as the width, usually longer; both grinding surfaces convex on both axes. Over-all shape that of Type 1b mano (Fig. 33 *e*). One specimen has finger grooves. Type 2b manos could be used in wide troughed Type 3a and 3b metates.

Material: Tuff (2), fine grained basalt (1), vesicular basalt (1).

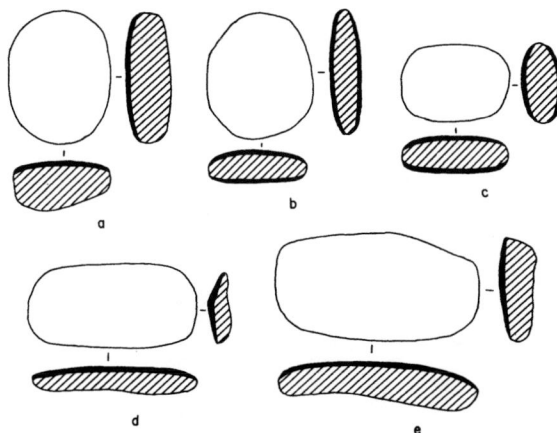

Fig. 33. Manos and handstones. *a*, mano, uniface, round to oval; *b*, mano, biface, round to oval; *c*, handstone, biface; *d*, mano, uniface, ridged; *e*, mano, uniface, rectangular. Heavy lines in cross-section indicate grinding surfaces. Length of *e*, 22.2 cm.

Provenience: Floor, Pithouses 5 (1), 6 (1); House fill, Pithouses 4 (1), 6 (1).

Handstones

Type 1. Six specimens; uniface; majority are well-shaped and rectangular; minority are ovoid; edges usually shaped; grinding surface flat to markedly convex on both axes. Over-all shape same as Type 2 handstones (Fig. 33 *c*). One is obviously right-handed; one has hammerstone batterings. Type 1 handstones could be used in Type 2 metates.

Material: Quartzite (3), fine-grained basalt (2).
Provenience: Floor, Pithouse 10 (1); Floor fill, Pithouse 4 (1); House fill, Pithouse 2 (1), 6 (1), 7 (1), 10 (1).

Type 2 (Fig. 33 *c*). Nineteen specimens; biface; oval to shaped rectangular; edges usually pecked; grinding surfaces flat to slightly convex on both axes. One has red pigment stain on grinding surface; one used as hammerstone on ends. Type 2 handstones could be used in Type 2 metates.

Material: Fine-grained basalt (8), quartzite (6), vesicular basalt (2), felsite (1), igneous (1), granite (1).
Provenience: Floor, Pithouses 1 (1), 8 (3); Floor fill, Pithouse 1 (2); House fill, Pithouses 3 (1), 4 (1), 5 (1), 8 (2), 9 (2), 10 (2), Great Kiva (1); Posthole fill, Great Kiva (1); Floor pit fill, Pithouse 8 (1), Great Kiva (1).

Pestles

Two specimens (Fig. 32 *b*); relatively short, squat tools; one well-shaped and other partially shaped; grinding surface convex on both axes. The illustrated specimen was found with the Type 1b grinding slab (Fig. 32 *a*).

Material: Fine-grained basalt (2).
Provenience: Fill, Storage pit, Pithouse 1 (1); House fill, Pithouse 6 (1).

Stone Bowls

Type 1a (Fig. 34 *f, g*). Two specimens; circular tuff bowls; one specimen finer-grained, better smoothed and has relatively deeper bowl depression; remnants of red pigment on exterior of other specimen.

Material: Tuff (2).
Provenience: Fill, northeast posthole, Pithouse 3 (2).

Type 1b (Fig. 34 *b*). Two specimens; hemispherical tuff bowls; not as well made as other stone bowls from site; surfaces uneven but smoothed; one specimen made from tuff geode.

Material: Tuff (2).

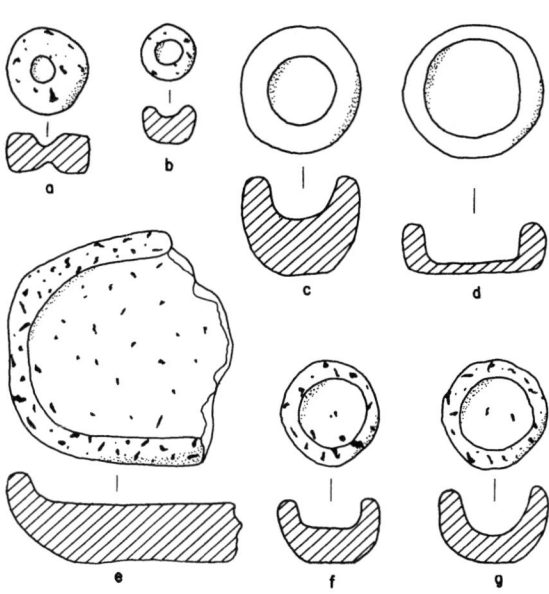

Fig. 34. Stone bowls, stone dish, and pitted tuff discoid. *a*, pitted tuff discoid; *b-d, f, g*, stone bowls; *e*, stone dish. Length of *e*, 13.2 cm.

Provenience: House fill, Pithouse 3 (1); Test 17 (1).

Type 2 (Fig. 34 d). One specimen; discoidal-shaped; symmetrical, polished, basin-shaped bowl depression; sides well polished; base flat and well polished.

Material: Fine-grained quartzite (1).
Provenience: Bottom of northeast posthole, Pithouse 1 (1).

Type 3 (Figs. 34 c, 35). One specimen; hemispherical; relatively straight-sided bowl-like depression; flat base; vertical stripes painted in red, yellow, and black, interspersed by stripes of unpainted stone. An occasional fleck of malachite on the unpainted stripes may indicate these areas were formerly green.

Material: Quartzite (1).
Provenience: Bottom of northeast posthole, Pithouse 1 (1).

Stone Dish

One specimen (Fig. 34 e); broken; edges shaped; dish depression rubbed smooth.

Material: Vesicular basalt (1).
Provenience: House fill, Pithouse 8 (1).

Pitted Tuff Discoids

Two specimens (Fig. 34 a); tuff pebbles ground to discoidal shape; upper and lower surfaces ground smoother than sides; conical pits in one specimen; rudimentary pits in other specimen.

Provenience: Fill, northeast posthole, Pithouse 3 (1); Floor fill, Pithouse 8 (1).

Stone Ring

Half of one complete specimen; circumference and sides rubbed flat; diameter of biconical perforation varies from 18 to 40 mm.; diameter of specimen, 94 mm.; thickness, 40 mm.; specimen has been burned.

Material: Tuff (1).
Provenience: House fill, Pithouse 3 (1).

Palettes

Type 1 (Fig. 36 a, b). Three specimens; fragments of Hohokam palettes; one specimen with shallow incised notches on outside border edge, another with running pattern of incised diamonds on border and pair of medial grooves.

Material: Schist (1), slate (1), unknown (1).

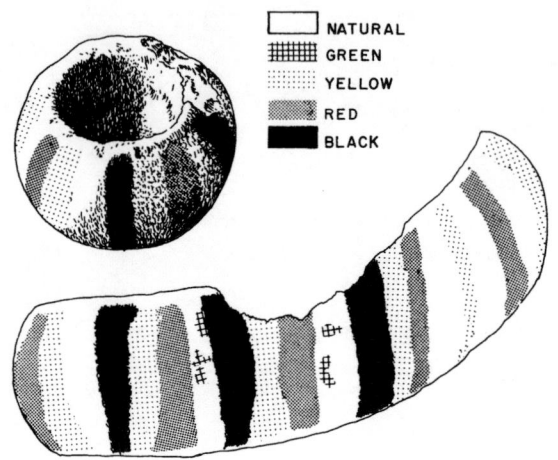

Fig. 35. Painted stone bowl. Sides rolled out to show sequence of decorated stripes. Diameter, 76 mm.

Provenience: Floor fill, Pithouse 9 (1); House fill, Pithouse 8 (1), Great Kiva (1).

Type 2 (Fig. 36 c). Two specimens; Mogollon type. One specimen oblong pebble palette with rectangular mixing surface outlined by incised lines; incised notches around circumference of pebble between mixing surface and edge; mixing surface has good polish. Other specimen microcrystalline; uniface with few shallow, irregular scratches on polished surface.

Material: Sandstone (1), microcrystalline (1).
Provenience: Floor fill, Pithouse 9 (1); House fill, Pithouse 8 (1).

Effigies

Type 1 (Fig. 36 d). One specimen; anthropomorphic(?); bifurcated base narrower than upper portions; pair of horizontal grooves encircle central portion; roundish head; shallow groove encircles specimen near top of head; one side of head has low prominence just below upper shallow groove; other side has vertical groove connecting upper shallow groove and uppermost of pair of horizontal grooves on body.

Material: Scoria (1).
Provenience: Floor trench, Great Kiva (1).

Type 2 (Fig. 36 e). One specimen; quadruped; resembles bear; two ears and one eye definite; slit mouth; anal depression.

Material: Tuff (1).
Provenience: Floor, Pithouse 1 (1).

PROBLEMATICAL STONE

One specimen (Fig. 36 *f*); cylindrical with enlarged, flattened end; shaped and ground; possibly phallic.

Material: Tuff (1).
Provenience: House fill, Pithouse 9 (1).

POLISHING STONES

Naturally shaped, fine-grained rocks selected for convenience; altered only by use. Two types are recognized on the basis of shape.

Type 1. Eleven specimens; small, elongate pebbles; microcrystalline; small, highly polished wear facets on face or broad edges; whole stone polished from being held in hand. Probably used in polishing pottery.

Material: Fine-grained basalts (9), light gray basalt (1), fine-grained quartzite (1).
Provenience: Floor, Pithouse 1 (1); Floor fill, Pithouses 1 (1), 3 (1), 5 (1); House fill, Pithouses 1 (1), 6 (1), 7 (1), 8 (1); Posthole fill, Pithouses 1 (1), 8 (1); Fill, storage pit, Pithouse 1 (1).

Type 2. Two fragmentary specimens; biface with flat faces polished.

Material: Microcrystalline 2.
Provenience: Floor fill, Pithouse 1 (2).

ABRADING STONES

Type 1. Six specimens; uniface; selected pebbles and cobbles; oval to rectangular in plan; oval, tabular or wedge-shaped in section; grinding surface flat to slightly convex; mostly irregular and shaped through use.

Material: Tuff (3), fine-grained basalt (1), quartzite (1), light, fine-grained igneous rock (1).
Provenience: Floor, Pithouse 5 (1); Floor fill, Pithouses 1 (1), 3 (1); House fill, Pithouse 5 (1); Floor pit, Pithouse 5 (1); Posthole fill, Great Kiva (1).

Type 2. Seven specimens; same as Type 1 except biface.

Material: Sandstone (4), scoria (2), fine-grained basalt (1).
Provenience: Floor fill, Pithouse 1 (1); House fill. Pithouses 4 (1), 5 (1), 6 (2), 7 (1); Pit fill, Pithouse 8 (1).

GROOVED ABRADING STONE

One specimen; shaped cobble, rectangular; transverse groove; grooved surface and one side ground.

Material: Limestone (1).
Provenience: House fill, Pithouse 4 (1).

SHAPED STONES

Two specimens; larger is loaf-shaped, no grinding evident, possibly mano blank; smaller is roughly rectangular with large rounded end rubbed along convex edge, possibly an axe blank.

Material: Vesicular basalt (1), fine-grained basalt (1).
Provenience: Floor, Pithouse 1 (1); Area northwest of Pithouse 10 (1).

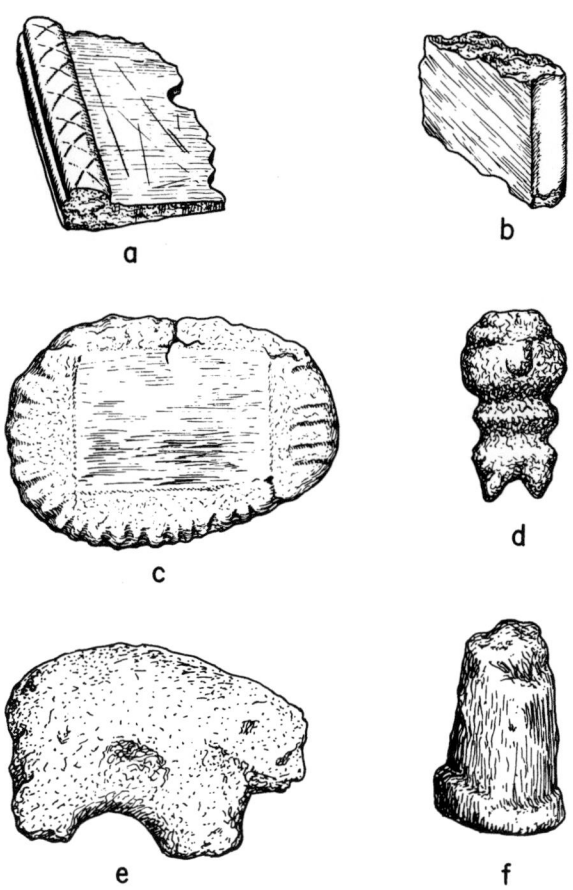

FIG. 36. Palettes, effigies, and problematical stone. *a, b,* Hohokam palettes; *c,* Mogollon palette; *d,* anthropomorphic(?) effigy; *e,* quadruped effigy; *f,* problematical stone. Length of *e,* 7.1 cm.

Hammerstones

Type 1. Sixty-seven specimens; used for hammering, pecking and percussion flaking; range from spherical to subangular; three show percussion flaking; several reduced almost to spheres through use; usually pecking evident around largest circumference and on prominences.

Material: Fine-grained basalt (20), quartz nodules (12), limestone (9), quartzite (5), chalcedony (4), rhyolite (4), felsite (4), tuff (3), fine-grained igneous (2), chert (2), vesicular basalt (1), porphyritic basalt (1).

Provenience: Floor, Pithouses 1 (11), 5 (2), 8 (3), Great Kiva (1); Posthole, Great Kiva (1); Floor fill, Pithouses 1 (4), 4 (1), 10 (2), Great Kiva (1); House fill, Pithouses 1 (7), 4 (2), 5 (2), 6 (5), 8 (3), 9 (12), 10 (6), Great Kiva (4).

Grooved Mauls

Three specimens; made from cobbles; seven-eighths grooved; ends rounded on two specimens, flattened on other; groove at center in two specimens, toward one end in other; one specimen has exfoliated side and very shallow groove.

Material: Vesicular basalt (1), fine-grained basalt (1), quartzite (1).

Provenience: Floor, Pithouse 8 (1); Floor of storage pit, Pithouse 1 (1); Floor fill, Pithouse 8 (1).

Provenience: Posthole fill, Great Kiva (1).

Grooved Tuff Cobble

One specimen (Fig. 37 *a*); irregularly ovoid tuff cobble with shallow, irregular full groove; simulates grooved maul in appearance but material and weight argue against such use except as toy. May have been used as a weight.

Three-Quarter Grooved Axes

Two specimens (Fig. 37 *b, c*); one much larger than other; highly polished; moderately deep three-quarter groove; gently curving sides and poll. Other specimen smaller with straighter sides; round poll.

Material: Coarse-grained andesite (2).

Provenience: Floor fill, Pithouse 3 (1); House fill, Pithouse 4 (1).

Ornaments

Disc Beads. Nine specimens; cylindrically perforated discs.

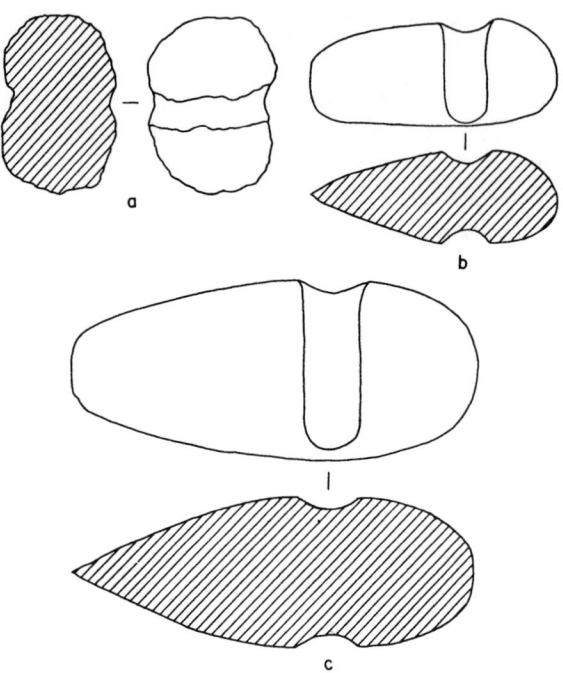

Fig. 37. Grooved tuff cobble and three-quarter grooved axes. *a,* grooved tuff cobble; *b, c,* three-quarter grooved axes. Length of *c,* 19.8 cm.

Material: Soapstone (4), phyllite (3), turquoise (2).
Provenience: Firepit, Pithouse 6 (1); Posthole fill, Great Kiva (2); Floor fill, Pithouse 1 (2); House fill, Pithouse 1 (1), 9 (1); Burial 2 (2).

Hematite Disc. One specimen; squarish, flat sheet of specular hematite naturally adhered to felspar which contains some quartz. Edges have been ground. Dimensions: length, 12 mm.; width, 11 mm.; thickness, 2 mm.

Provenience: Surface of site (1).

Minerals

Hematite. Found frequently in house fill. Six specimens have abrasion facets. Red pigment stains on grinding tools probably hematite.

Clay Nodules. Two white clay nodules believed to be for manufacture of white paint were found on the floor of Pithouse 1.

Quartz Crystals. Two single quartz crystals and one twin crystal were recorded.

Chalcedony Nodule. One Desert Rose. Surface.

Malachite, Obsidian Nodules, Azurite and Limonite. Miscellaneous specimens found in house fill.

CURIOS

Crinoid Stem. House fill, Pithouse 3.

Petrified Wood. One chip from Petrified Forest National Monument region. Pithouse 6.

Tuff Geodes. Floor fill, Pithouse 3 (1); House fill, Pithouse 9 (1); Great Kiva (1).

Tear-shaped Chalcedony Pebble. House fill, Pithouse 6.

DISCUSSION

During field excavation a tabulation of incomplete stone tools was made for comparison with complete artifacts. This category, designated Field Noted Stone, generally corroborates the ratios of artifact groupings in the preceding section. Thirty-four metate fragments show basically the same types, and ratios between types, as seen in the whole specimens. Fragments of 112 manos and handstones and seven grinding slabs show the same general ratio of uniface to biface types. The only point of discrepancy is the abrading stones, which show 19 uniface fragments as compared to 10 incomplete biface specimens.

Metates are of four types: flat boulder, full basin, closed-end trough, and "Utah." Basin and closed-end trough, or scoop, metates are by far the most popular types, the latter being preponderant. Boulders for metates are generally selected for shape and size and altered through use. The "Utah" type metate from the floor of Pithouse 6 indicates that this unit is a relatively early Nantack Phase dwelling. Metates are in floor contact or in floor pits in all semi-subterranean units except Pithouses 2, 4, and 9. Number of metates in floor contact ranges from 1 to 7.

Grinding slabs are arbitrarily separated from metates on the basis of their smaller size and generally shallower grinding surfaces. Half of the six grinding slabs recovered are re-used manos. The presence of red pigment on the grinding surface of two of the small grinding slabs indicates that these artifacts are not for preparing food. One of the two pestles was found in association with a small, mano-like grinding slab.

Manos are preponderantly uniface and shaped. Types 1b and 2b, uniface and biface rectangular, could be used effectively in Type 3, troughed, metates. Biface manos are similar to the uniface types in over-all shape and configurations of the grinding surfaces. The presence of two instead of one grinding surface is the only criterion for differentiation.

Handstones are smaller, broader and thicker than manos. They could be used on basin metates or grinding slabs. Handstones are consistently well-shaped and the ratio of uniface to biface is the opposite of that for manos.

Five of the six stone bowls are from two units, Pithouses 1 and 3. Four of these are from the northeast, main support posthole, but as the trait does not recur in other pithouses no cultural connotation is hypothesized. The single example of a painted stone bowl (Figs. 34c, 35) conforms to similar specimens from the Reserve Region. Martin reports a cache of Mogollon ceremonial artifacts from Higgins Flat Pueblo. One of the artifacts is a stone bowl painted red, yellow, black, and green (Martin 1954: 3–4). The flecks of malachite adhering to the unpainted portions of the stone bowl from Nantack Village indicate that these four colors were used together in both Mogollon regions. The four stone bowls which have the poorest workmanship are made from local tuff. The painted and the discoidal, polished bowls are importations into Nantack Village.

The fragmentary stone dish is made of vesicular basalt and local manufacture is postulated.

Pitted tuff discoids or pitted pebbles made of local material are also reported by Wheat (1954: 118). Their place in the artifact inventory is not known.

Three palettes have techniques and materials associated with the Sacaton Phase at Snaketown. They indicate contact with the Gila-Salt Basin during the Nantack Phase. The incised, pebble palette is a Mogollon artifact. It is not made from a locally occurring material but its place of origin is not known.

The anthropomorphic(?) effigy of scoria resembles a human figurine from San Simon

Village (Sayles 1945, Pl. 49, *d*). The tuff quadruped effigy is made of local tuff. Martin reports two tuff bears(?) from the cache of ceremonial artifacts at Higgins Flat Pueblo (Martin 1954: 3–4; Martin and others 1956: 96, 125). The Reserve region specimens are painted but there is no indication that the bear(?) from the floor of Pithouse 1 was ever decorated.

Polishing stones are consistently microcrystalline pebbles altered through use. They are generally thought to be used in the smoothing and polishing of pottery vessels manufactured by the coil and scrape method.

An abrading stone is any corrosive pebble or cobble which can be used to abrade. They are generally unshaped and altered through use. However, the single specimen of a grooved abrading stone shows purposeful shaping.

Hammerstones used until all angular edges are battered off become roughly spherical balls. Two of the most common uses for hammerstones are for sharpening metates and for use in percussion flaking.

The three mauls are specialized, hafted, hammerstones.

The grooved tuff pebble resembles a maul but it is made from the light and soft local leucite tuff which is ineffective for battering. Its small size also makes its postulated use as a weight instead of a maul seem logical.

The two three-quarter grooved axes have material and method of manufacture indigenous in the Hohokam area.

The sporadic occurrence of stone, disc beads indicates personal ornamentation. The variety of material represented bespeaks of trade with surrounding regions.

The ground-edged disc of specular hematite is an unusual specimen. It is possibly a portion of a mosaic or mirror.

Utilitarian and esthetic values are both expressed in the miscellaneous minerals and curios from Nantack Village. Pithouse 6 has more of these objects than any other single unit. This, plus the conglomeration of ground stone tools on the floor, may indicate that the inhabitants of Pithouse 6 had a flair for collecting unusual specimens, natural and man-made.

FLAKED STONE

Flaked stone artifacts from the Nantack Phase occupation are classified as follows:

	Individual Types	Total
Projectile points		38
Unstemmed		
Type 1, triangular	3	
Stemmed		
Type 2a, diagonal notches	4	
Type 2b, diagonal notches, small	4	
Type 3, diagonal notches, straight stem, small	3	
Type 4, expanding stem, straight base	1	
Type 5a, tapering stem, convex base	4	
Type 5b, tapering stem, concave base	1	
Side notched		
Type 6, shallow side notches	3	
Type 7, deep side notches, convex base	1	
Type 8, side notches, concave base	4	
Type 9a, side notches, straight base	6	
Type 9b, side notches, straight base, small	3	
Type 10, side notches, tapering stem	1	
Knives		25
Type 1, flake knives	10	
Type 2, leaf-shaped	10	
Type 3, notched	1	
Type 4, bubbled chalcedony	2	
Type 5, flow basalt	2	
Drills		3
Type 1, shaped base	2	
Type 2, unshaped base	1	
Scrapers		6
Type 1, nosed	2	
Type 2, side	4	
Flake gravers		3
Blades-saws		10
Stone disc		1
Choppers		3
Total		89

PROJECTILE POINTS

Blade proportions for projectile points refer to the width relative to the length of the blade.

Unstemmed

Type 1, Triangular (Fig. 38 *a, b*). Three specimens; one point with straight base and edges; one with convex base and straight edges; one with concave base and slightly convex edges. All flaked on one side only.

Material: Obsidian (2), chert (1).
Provenience: House fill, Pithouse 9 (1), Great Kiva (1); Surface (1).

Stemmed

Type 2a, Diagonal notches (Fig. 38 *c*). Four specimens; medium size; blades of medium proportions; edges slightly to moderately convex; shoulders prominent and wider than base; stem moderately to widely expanded; base straight to convex. One has sharply contracting tip which may be a drill.

Material: Obsidian (2), jasper (1), chert (1).
Provenience: Floor fill, Pithouses 1 (1), 5 (1); Area northwest of Pithouse 10 (1); Surface (1).

Type 2b, Diagonal notches, small (Fig. 38 *d*). Four specimens; differ from Type 2a by smaller size, stem less expanding and more slender proportioned blades. Two show wear on edges near tip with offset which may be intended to serve as drill tips rather than projectiles. Two chipped on one side only.

Material: Obsidian (3), chert (1).
Provenience: Surface (2); Pithouses 5 (1), 7 (1).

Type 3, Diagonal notches, straight stem, small (Fig. 38 *e, f*). Three specimens; blades of medium proportions; shoulders prominent to barbed and wider than stem; stem straight and narrow.

Material: Obsidian (3).
Provenience: Floor fill, Pithouse 1 (1); House fill, Pithouse 10 (1); Surface (1).

Type 4, Expanding stem, straight base. One specimen; tip missing; prominent shoulder wider than base; base straight.

Material: Chert (1).
Provenience: Surface (1).

Type 5a, Tapering stem, convex base (Fig. 38 *h-j*). Four specimens; blades of slender to broad proportions; edges straight to slightly convex; shoulders slight to prominent. Three show wear on edges at tip with offset which may be intended to serve as drill tips rather than projectiles.

Material: Obsidian (4).
Provenience: House fill, Pithouse 6 (1); Backdirt, Pithouse 3 (1); Surface (2).

Type 5b, Tapering stem, concave base (Fig. 38 *g*). One specimen; blade of medium proportions; edges slightly concave; stem tapering; base concave.

Material: Chert (1).
Provenience: House fill, Pithouse 9 (1).

Side Notched

Type 6, Shallow side notches (Fig. 38 *k*). Three specimens; blades of medium proportions; side notches shallow; edges slightly convex; base straight.

Material: Obsidian (2). chert (1).
Provenience: House fill, Pithouses 1 (1), 9 (1); Surface (1).

Type 7, Deep side notches, convex base (Fig. 38 *l*). One specimen; blade of broad proportions; edges irregular; side notches deep; prominent shoulder wider than base; base convex.

Material: Obsidian (1).
Provenience: Surface (1).

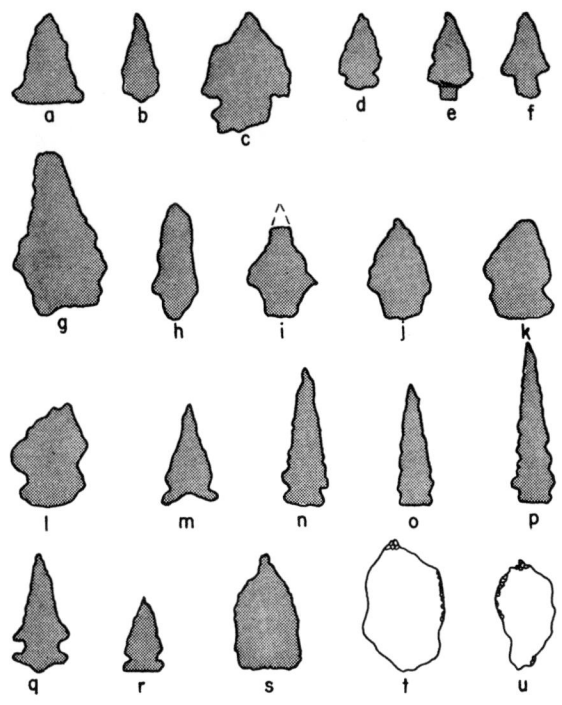

FIG 38. Projectile points, drill, and flake gravers. *a-r*, projectile points; *s*, drill; *t, u*, flake gravers. Stipple indicates all-over chipping. Length of *g*, 43 mm.

Type 8, Side notches, concave base (Fig. 38 *m*). Four specimens; blades of slender to moderate proportions; edges straight; side notches deep and wide; bases concave and wider than shoulders. One has three serrations anterior to the side notches.

Material: Obsidian (4).
Provenience: Floor, Pithouse 1 (1); House fill, Great Kiva (1); Backdirt, Pithouse 7 (1); Surface (1).

Type 9a, Side notches, straight base (Fig. 38 *n-p*). Six specimens; blades of slender proportions; three have serrations on basal half of blade; edges and base straight.

Material: Obsidian (6).
Provenience: Floor fill, Pithouse 1 (1); House fill, Pithouses 1 (1), 6 (1), 9 (1), 10 (1); Surface (1).

Type 9b, Side notches, straight base, small (Fig. 38 *r*). Three specimens; differ from Type 9a by consistently smaller size and broader blade proportions; shoulders prominent and wider than base except in one specimen.

Material: Obsidian (3).
Provenience: House fill, Pithouse 6 (1); Surface (2).

Type 10, Side notches, tapering stem (Fig. 38 *q*). One specimen; blade slender; edges straight; two wide shoulders separated by side notch; stem short and tapering.

Material: Obsidian (1).
Provenience: House fill, Pithouse 8 (1).

KNIVES

Some of the artifacts classified as projectile points could be used as small, hafted knives. Bifacially chipped blades thought to be knives are classified as follows:

Type 1, Flake knives (Fig. 39 *a*). Ten specimens; rough, random flakes; rectangular to irregular; crude bifacial flaking or use-scars form cutting edge around one-quarter to two-thirds of margin.

Material: Chert (4), obsidian (2), quartzite (2), chalcedony (1), fine-grained basalt (1).
Provenience: Floor fill, Pithouses 1 (2), 4 (1), 5 (1), 10 (1); House fill, Pithouses 1 (1), 3 (2), 4 (2).

Type 2, Leaf-shaped (Fig. 39 *b*). Ten specimens; small, leaf-shaped knives; larger relative thickness, general asymmetry and absence of

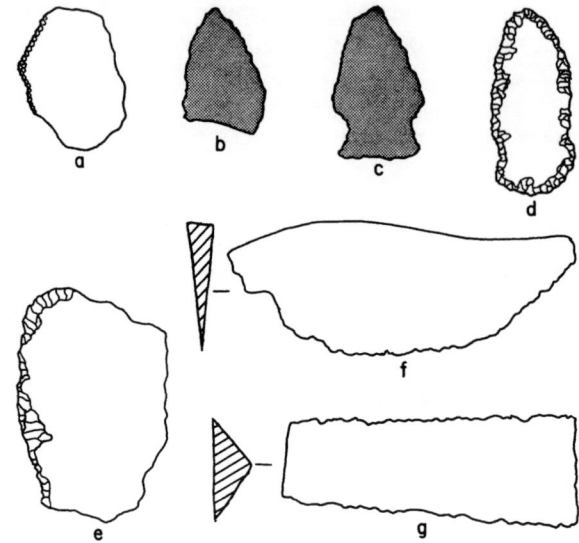

Fig. 39. Knives. *a,* flake knife; *b,* leaf-shaped knife; *c,* notched knife; *d, e,* bubbled chalcedony; *f, g,* flow basalt. Stipple indicates all-over chipping. Length of *g,* 80 mm.

stems or notches differentiates them from projectile points; cutting edge flakes bifacially around perimeter of complete specimens.

Material: Chert (5), quartzite (2), jasper (1), obsidian (1), chalcedony (1).
Provenience: Floor, Pithouse 6 (1); House fill, Pithouses 1 (1), 3 (1), 10 (1); Backdirt, Pithouse 1 (1); Test 2C (1); Surface (4).

Type 3, Notched (Fig. 39 *c*). One specimen; blade moderately broad; edges slightly convex; side notches broad and shallow; base straight. Size and material differentiates this specimen from Type 6 projectile points.

Material: Basalt (1).
Provenience.: House fill, Great Kiva (1).

Type 4, Bubbled chalcedony (Fig. 39 *d, e*). Two specimens; one oblong with shallow side notches and bifacial chipping around all edges; other subrectangular with bifacially chipped, slightly convex, single cutting edge..

Provenience: Floor fill, Pithouse 1 (2).

Type 5, Flow basalt (Fig. 39 *f, g*). Two specimens; one semi-lunar with convex cutting edge, triangular in section; other with double, straight cutting edges and prominent longitudinal ridge.

Provenience: Floor fill, Pithouse 1 (2).

DRILLS

Type 1, Shaped base (Fig. 38 *s*). Two specimens; straight, well-chipped base; possibly reworked projectile points; shafts relatively short and tapering; shafts round in section.

Material: Obsidian (2).
Provenience: House fill, Pithouse 7 (1); Surface (1).

Type 2, Unshaped base (Fig. 40 *c*). One specimen; random flake base; shaft straight with round tip; shaft oval in section.

Material: Jasper (1).
Provenience: Backdirt, Great Kiva (1).

SCRAPERS

Type 1, Nosed (Fig. 40 *b*). Two specimens; small, thick, elongated percussion flakes; unifacially retouched along sides and point; scraping point low angled, under 45 degrees.

Material: Chalcedony (1), chert (1).
Provenience: Floor fill, Pithouse 5 (1); House fill, Pithouse 5 (1).

Type 2, Side (Fig. 40 *a*). Four specimens; thickened percussion flakes; retouched around approximately one-third of side or end.

Material: Chert (2), quartz (1), basalt (1).
Provenience: Floor fill, Pithouse 10 (1); House fill, Pithouse 7 (1); Burial 1 (1); Surface (1).

FLAKE GRAVERS

Three specimens (Fig. 38 *t, u*); small, curved flakes with use marks concentrated at tip. Some use-chipping along sides of flakes.

Material: Obsidian (3).
Provenience: Floor fill, Pithouse 5 (2); Surface (1).

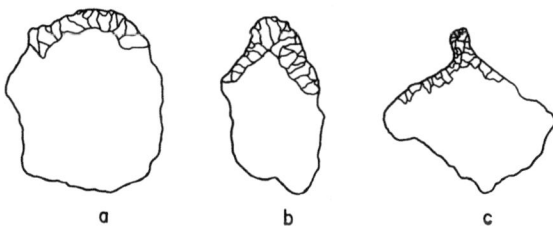

FIG. 40. Scrapers and drill. *a*, side scraper; *b*, nosed scraper; *c*, drill, unshaped base. Length of *a*, 40 mm.

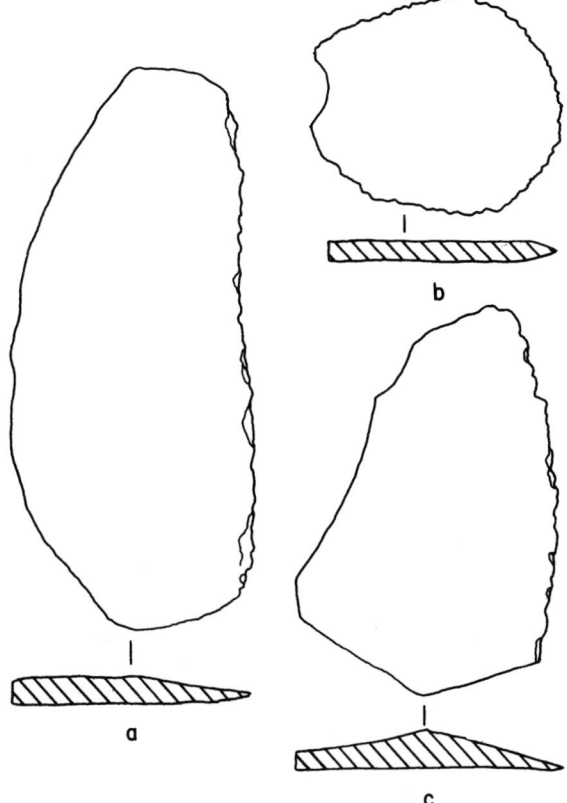

FIG. 41. Blades-saws and chipped disc. *a, c,* blades-saws; *b,* chipped disc. Length of *a,* 17.6 cm.

BLADES-SAWS

Ten specimens (Fig. 41 *a, c*); tabular plates of flow basalt; triangular in section; one with longitudinal ridge; single-edged (7) or double-edged (3); retouched to produce cutting edge; cutting edge straight (4), convex (4), or concave (2). Two have red pigment stain on one surface. Two specimens have use striations which indicate use as knives or saws; no use striations on other specimens.

Material: Flow basalt (10).
Provenience: Floor, Pithouse 5 (2); Floor fill, Pithouse 1 (2); House fill, Pithouses 1 (2), 4 (1), 6 (1), 8 (1), 9 (1).

STONE DISC

One specimen (Fig. 41 *b*); thin disc of flow basalt; retouched around entire circumference except for broken end. Could be used as knife, or

possibly is pendant with perforation at broken end.
Provenience: Posthole, Great Kiva (11.

CHOPPERS

Three specimens; oval to irregular; cutting edge produced by striking percussion flakes from cobble; other portion of cobble unaltered except one specimen which shows evidence of use as a hammerstone.
Material: Chert (1), felsite (1), limestone (1).
Provenience: Floor, Pithouse 5 (3).

DISCUSSION

Projectile points constitute the largest category of flaked stone tools from Nantack Village. No more than six of any one type are recorded. Stemmed and side notched categories are almost equally popular. Evidence of grinding at the tip of six specimens may indicate that these artifacts are drills. Obsidian is the overwhelming choice of material for projectile points. Some of the 38 artifacts classified as projectile points could be used equally well as hafted knives or scrapers. Fourteen projectile points are from the surface and their assignment to the Nantack Phase is tenuous.

Flake knives could be quickly manufactured from any suitable random flake. Their size and shape are variable. Leaf-shaped knives are perhaps unhafted projectile points. The two knives fashioned from sheets of bubbled chalcedony may be trade items. Alan P. Olson informs me that a similar type of chalcedony occurs in the Reserve region.

Three definite drills are noted. One of the drills is a reworked projectile point.

The small number of scrapers may indicate that the residents of Nantack Village utilized bone, wood or other perishable materials for scraping tools. There is no consistency in the typological characteristics of the six scrapers and the categories are arbitrary.

Flake gravers are more numerous than indicated by the three recorded specimens. These small, curved flakes of obsidian were not recognized as artifacts until late in the excavation of the site. The concentration of use or pressure flaking at the tips of these artifacts suggests use as graving or incising tools.

The ten blades-saws are no doubt multi-function tools. The working edge was produced by percussion or pressure flaking. Two of the specimens show evidence of use as saws or knives. Eight blades-saws do not have longitudinal wear facets on the working edge and they are perhaps thin choppers, hoes or skinning knives. The presence of red pigment on two specimens indicates an additional use of the blades-saws as paint palettes.

The three choppers, produced by rough percussion flaking, might be better classified as unused hammerstones.

As in the case of ground stone artifacts, incomplete specimens of flaked stone tools were recorded in the field. Flaked stone artifacts so noted are: four flake knives, three scrapers, one flake graver, three blades-saws, one chopper, and three cores. Except for two of the cores, from the floor of Pithouse 5, none of the field noted flaked stone tools were found in floor contact.

BONE, ANTLER AND SHELL ARTIFACTS

There are few artifacts of bone, antler and shell from Nantack Village. Most of the bone artifacts are made from deer long bones. Shell artifacts indicate trade directly or indirectly with the Gulf of California or the Pacific Ocean.

Artifacts of bone, antler and shell are classified as follows:

Bone awls
  Awls, articular head unmodified 5
    Type 1, ulna 1
    Type 2, metatarsus, notched 1
  Awls, articular head modified by splitting
    Type 3a, metatarsus, unnotched, long 1
    Type 3b, metatarsus, unnotched, short.... 2
Bone ring blanks 2

THE NANTACK PHASE

Bone ring fragment	1
Bone hair ornament(?)	1
Antler tube	1
Shell pendant	1
Shell bracelet and fragments	7
Shell ring fragment	1
Shell fragment, *Pecten,* unworked	1
Disc bead	1
Total	21

BONE

AWLS

Type 1, Deer ulna (Fig. 42 *f*). One specimen; distal end ground to point; length, 131 mm.

Provenience: House fill, Pithouse 3 (1).

Type 2, Deer metatarsus, notched (Fig. 42 *g*). One specimen; short awl with notch near articular end; length, 86 mm.

Provenience: House fill, Pithouse 1 (1).

Type 3a, Long, unnotched (Fig. 42 *e*). One specimen; made from distal end of deer metatarsus; slender; highly polished; length 245 mm.

Provenience: Test 3D.

Type 3 b, Short, unnotched (Fig. 42 *h, i*). Two specimens; one made from distal end of deer metatarsus, evenly tapered to point; other from immature deer metatarsus. Lengths, 104 and 115 mm.

Provenience: Floor fill, Pithouse 1 (1); House fill, Pithouse 5 (1).

MISCELLANEOUS

Bone Ring Blanks. Two specimens; section of long bone shaft of deer or other large mammals from which bone rings have been cut. Length of measured specimen, 46 mm.

Provenience: Floor and House fill, Pithouse 1 (2).

Bone Ring Fragment. One specimen; approximately one-third of cut and polished bone ring; width, 5 mm.; thickness, 2 mm.

Provenience: House fill, Pithouse 7 (1).

Bone Hair Ornament(?) (Fig. 42 *b*). One specimen; flat, highly polished section of mammal long bone; evidence of right angle cut; length, 108 mm.; width, 31 mm.

Provenience: House fill, Pithouse 5 (1).

ANTLER

Antler Tube (Fig. 42 *a*). One specimen; section of hollowed antler; one end broken during excavation; evidence of rodent gnawing on exterior; length, 80 mm.; diameter, 19 mm.; perforation, average diameter, 5 mm.

Provenience: Floor fill, Pithouse 8 (1).

SHELL

Shell Pendant (Fig. 42 *d*). One specimen; roughly oval, curved piece of *Laevicardium elatum* Sowerby; biconical perforation; length, 29

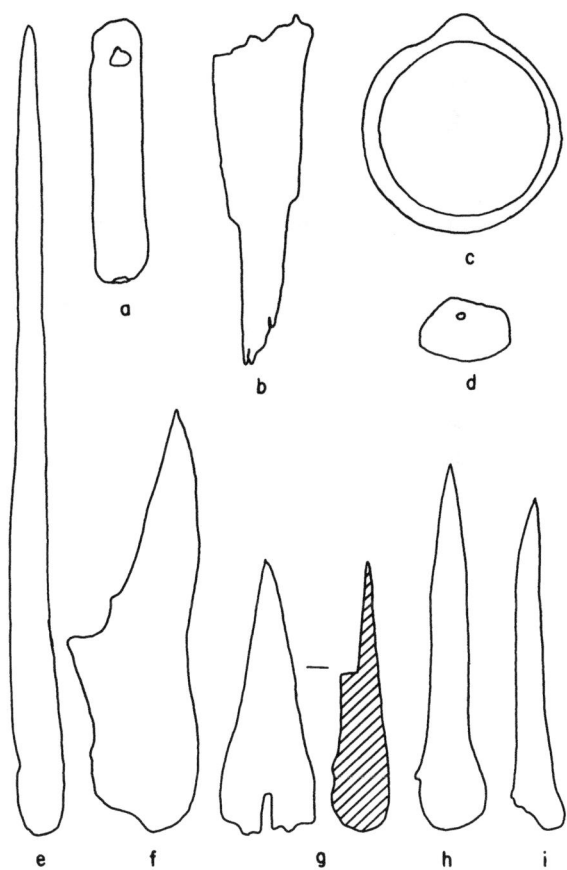

FIG. 42. Bone, antler, and shell artifacts. *a,* antler tube; *b,* bone hair ornament(?); *c, Glycymeris* shell bracelet; *d,* shell pendant; *e,* bone awl, metatarsus, unnotched, long; *f,* bone awl, deer ulna; *g,* bone awl, deer metatarsus,, notched; *h, i,* bone awls, deer metatarsus, unnotched, short. Length of *e,* 24.5 cm.

mm.; width, 20 mm.; thickness, 2.5 mm.; diameter of perforation 2 mm.

Provenience: Floor fill, Pithouse 8 (1).

Shell Bracelet and Fragments (Fig. 42 c). One complete specimen and six fragments, thin ground, polished; made of *Glycymeris* valves; whole specimen and one fragment have remnants of incised parallel lines around perimeter of bracelet. Dimensions of complete specimen; diameter, 63 mm.; width, 9 mm.; diameter of perforation, 2 mm.

Provenience of complete specimen: Burial 2.

Shell Ring Fragment. One specimen; highly polished section of cut shell; species unidentifiable; width, 4 mm.; thickness, 3 mm.

Provenience: Backdirt, Great Kiva (1).

Shell Fragment, Unworked. One specimen, *Pecten.*

Provenience: House fill, Pithouse 5 (1).

Disc Bead. One specimen; small, ground; cylindrical perforation.

Provenience: Floor pit, Pithouse 7 (1).

Discussion

Bone, antler and shell artifacts are notably few in number. The five bone awls, the bone ring fragment and the bone hair ornament(?) are all highly polished. The polish produced during manufacture and through use probably acted as a preserving factor for the specimens.

Bone ring blanks are the discarded waste resulting from the manufacture of bone rings or bone tubes. Bone rings are separated from the shafts of mammal long bones by means of transverse cuts, but occasionally incompletely severed bone rings are still intact on the ring blanks. The polished fragment of a bone ring is the finished artifact of this process.

The possible hair ornament is a flat, highly polished section from a mammal long bone with a right angle cut.

The antler tube is incomplete and a roughly cylindrical, longitudinal perforation is the only human alteration.

Shell is an intrusive material at Nantack Village. The species represented are from the Gulf of California or the Pacific Ocean. The complete and fragmentary *Glycymeris* bracelets were made in a typical Hohokam fashion and were probably brought into Nantack Village as finished products.

SYNOPSIS OF THE NANTACK PHASE

The Nantack Phase is assigned to the Mogollon 4 period, A.D. 900-1000, in Point of Pines prehistory. There are no dendrochronological dates and the time period has been established by the presence of intrusive pottery and by comparison of the material culture and architectural data from Nantack Village with adjacent regions.

The excavated semi-subterranean pithouses are typically rectangular with lateral entryways. Six main post holes, indicating a flat or low gabled roof, is the most common pattern. The hearth is clay-rimmed with a sub-hearth depression.

The Nantack Phase Great Kiva is the largest Mogollon structure excavated to date. The ten large post holes are asymmetrically positioned and suggest a flat roof.

The ceramic complex is generally comparable to other Mogollon 4 phases and specifically similar to the Three Circle Phase. Intrusive pottery is present from all adjacent regions except the west.

Lithic artifacts are generally similar to other Mogollon 4 materials.

Trait List

The following trait list is a summary of the material culture excavated from the pithouses and tests at Nantack Village. The terms used to indicate relative occurrences, i.e., rare, present and common, are subjective and based on numbers of artifacts analyzed. Some of the artifacts are undoubtedly multi-function implements. Functional connotations are implied and frequently have been specifically mentioned with the description of the artifacts. Asterisks (*) denote traits or trait complexes considered diagnostic for the Nantack Phase. Question marks (?) indicate that association with the Nantack Phase is questionable.

Domestic Architecture
   Shape   *Rectangular
   Entrance
      Orientation .... *North to east quadrant
      Ramp with terminal step .... Present
      Stepped .... Present
   Wall features
      Recess opposite entry .... Present
      Wall niche .... Rare
      Peripheral rocks .... Present
   Floor
      Plastered .... *Common
      Catch basin .... Rare
   Hearth
      Rock-lined .... *Common
      Clay-lined .... Present
   Pits
      Within pithouse .... *Common
      Outside pithouse .... Present
   Roofing
      6 main supports .... *Common
      Recessed in pairs .... *Common
   Evidence of burning .... Present
   Evidence of reoccupation .... Present

Ceremonial Architecture
    This is based on the features of the Great Kiva and an assumed ceremonial connotation for Pithouse 10.
   Shape .... Rectangular
   Entrance .... Step in Great Kiva
      Orientation .... East, in Great Kiva
   Floor
      Plaster evidence .... In Great Kiva
      Warming basin or oven ...... Possibly, for both units
   Hearth .... Not definitely located
   Pits
      Within structure .... In both units
      Outside structure .... In Pithouse 10
      Deep (over 28 cm.) .... In both units
   Roofing
      10 main supports .... In both units
      Recessed in pairs .... In Pithouse 10
      Asymmetrical .... In Great Kiva

Ceramics
   Decorated and Textured types
     *Encinas Red-on-brown
     *Sacaton Red-on-buff
     *Sacanton Red-on-buff, Safford Variety
     *Mangas Black-on-white
     *PII "Northern" black-on-whites
     *Three Circle Neck Corrugated
     *Pine Flat Neck Corrugated
     *Reserve Indented Corrugated

   Plain and Redware types
     *Alma Plain, Point of Pines Variety
     *San Francisco Red, Point of Pines Variety
     *Reserve Red, Point of Pines Variety
   Ceramic artifacts
      Quadruped figurines .... Rare
      Perforated sherd discs .... *Common
      Unperforated sherd discs .... Common
      Sherd scrapers .... Present
      Incised sherds .... Rare
      Ceramic tubes .... Rare(?)
      Duck effigy vessels .... Rare(?)

Ground Stone
   Metates
      Flat slab .... Rare
      Full basin .... Common
      Closed-end trough (scoop) .. *Common
      "Utah" type .... Rare
   Grinding slabs
      Uniface, unshaped .... Present
      Uniface, shaped .... Rare
      Biface, shaped .... Present
   Manos
      Uniface, round to oval .... *Common
      Uniface, rectangular .... *Common
      Uniface, ridged .... Rare
      Biface, round to oval .... *Common
      Biface, rectangular .... Present
   Handstones
      Uniface .... Present
      Biface .... *Common
   Pestles .... Present
   Stone bowls
      Painted .... Rare
      Unpainted .... Present
   Stone dishes .... Rare
   Pitted tuff discoids .... Present
   Stone rings .... Rare
   Palettes
      Hohokam .... Present
      Mogollon .... Present
   Effigies
      Anthropomorphic(?) .... Rare(?)
      Quadruped .... Rare
   Polishing stones .... Common
      Abrading stones .... Common
   Grooved abrading stones .... Rare
   Hammerstones .... *Common
   Full and ⅞ grooved mauls .... Present
   Grooved tuff cobbles .... Rare
   Three-quarter grooved axes .... Rare
   Ornaments
      Disc beads .... Present
      Hematite disc .... Rare(?)

Flaked Stone
- Projectile points
  - Unstemmed .... Present
  - Stemmed .... *Common
  - Side-notched .... *Common
- Knives
  - Flake knives .... Common
  - Leaf-shaped .... Common
  - Notched .... Rare
  - Tabular material .... Present
- Drills .... Present
- Scrapers .... Present
- Flake gravers .... Present
- Blades-saws .... Common
- Chipped stone discs .... Rare
- Choppers .... Present

Bone
- Awls
  - Articular head unmodified.... Present
  - Articular head split .... Present
  - Bone ring blanks..................... Present
  - Bone rings................................. Rare
  - Bone hair ornaments.............. Rare

Antler
- Antler tubes .... Rare

Shell
- *Glycymeris* bracelets............. Present
- Rings .... Rare
- Pendants .... Rare
- Beads .... Rare

3

THE POST-NANTACK PHASE OCCUPATION

SINCE THE primary purpose of this report is a definition of the Nantack Phase the post-Nantack material from Nantack Village is not emphasized. However, six rooms belonging to the Reserve and Tularosa phases and several architectural features not assigned to a phase were dug.

Short discussions attempt to point out differences in material culture of the Nantack and Reserve-Tularosa phases. Architecture, ceramics, and to a lesser extent, stone tools, associated with the post-Nantack occupation of the site differ from the Nantack Phase material.

ARCHITECTURE

Three of the six excavated surface rooms at Nantack Village are a contiguous-roomed unit, designated Room B. Portions of two of its rooms overlie Pithouse 4.

The other three excavated surface rooms are located near the north end of the ridge and are designated Ruin C. The three rooms in Ruin C *are not* contiguous and do not necessarily belong to the same time period.

In 1954 a series of boulder alignments at the south end of the site, designated Ruin A, were tested. Work was stopped when no dwelling units could be defined.

Ruin B

Illustrations: Fig. 6.

Shape: All three rooms roughly rectangular.

Dimensions: (inside wall measurements) Short dimension of rooms, 2.60 m. to 3.00 m.; long dimensions, 3.05 m. to 4.05 m. Depth from present surface, 0.15 to 0.50 m.

Construction: All walls are "core-and-rubble."

The bottom course of masonry is a core of partially shaped basalt or shaped tuff boulders faced with approximately 0.10 m. of pebbles and copious amounts of mud. The second course is a layer of pebbles and cobbles set in mud. Only Room 3 has a third course, which is like the first (Fig. 43).

The scarcity of rock in the fill of all three rooms suggests that the low core-and-rubble masonry is the base for an upper wall of jacal. All walls range from 0.25 to 0.30 m. in thickness.

The three rooms are contemporaneous. Rooms 1 and 2 have a common northwest wall and Rooms 1 and 3 have a common northeast wall. The southeast wall of Room 2 is bonded with the southwest wall of Room 3 and the common wall between Rooms 1 and 2 (Fig. 6).

Entrances: No outside entrances located. A possible intramural doorway between Rooms 1 and 3 is suggested by a missing core boulder at the south corner of Room 1 and hard packed floor

Fig. 43. Ruin B, Room 3, wall detail. Core-and-rubble masonry with mud-pebble-cobble veneer.

in both rooms at this point.

Floors: Room 1: Irregular, part on native soil and part on trashy fill. East corner is built over Pithouse 4. Room 2: On trash which contains tuff inclusions; floor area southeast of hearth lower than rest of floor. Room 3: On trash and poorly defined. Western two-thirds built over Pithouse 4.

Hearths: Room 1: Circular clay basin partly rimmed with basalt rocks. Room 2: Rectangular, lined with sandstone slabs on three sides; sandstone slab in bottom of hearth. Room 3: Tuff-lined basin rimmed with basalt cobbles.

Pits: None located.

Postholes: None located.

Other floor features: Room 1: Alma Plain sherd plastered into floor in depressed east corner indicates presence of milling area. Room 2: Reserve Indented Corrugated sherd plastered into wall and grinding slab on floor near the east corner indicates a milling area. Room 3: No built-in milling features, but fragment of mano and metate from the floor near the east corner may indicate that this is, again, a milling area.

Material culture on floor: Room 1: mano fragment; 1 Alma Plain bowl sherd plastered into floor. Room 2: 1 basin metate, 1 grinding slab, 1 perforated sherd disc; 1 Reserve Indented Corrugated jar sherd plastered into wall. Room 3: 1 blade-saw, 2 metate fragments, 1 mano fragment, 2 perforated sherd discs.

Phase assignment: Tularosa Phase.

Remarks: All three rooms of Ruin B have architectural features found in the Tularosa Phase at Point of Pines. These include: use of facing on masonry walls; variation in hearth type; section of room associated with food grinding activities.

Ruin C

Room 1

Illustrations: Fig. 44, 45.

Shape: Roughly square with convex east and west walls.

Dimensions: North-south, 2.30 m.; east-west, 1.85 m. to 2.40 m. Depth from present surface, 0.45 to 0.55 m.

Construction: The east, south and west walls are large unshaped tuff and basalt boulders set on approximately 0.25 m. of trashy fill. Average thickness of these walls is 0.25 to 0.35 m. The east wall is built above and partly over the west wall of Ruin C, Room 3.

The north wall of Ruin C, Room 1 rests on yellow native clay and is two courses of relatively large boulders and small pebbles of tuff and basalt. The wall is 0.35 m. thick and continues as the north wall of Ruin B, Room 3. The technique of construction is *not* the same as the core-and-rubble of Ruin B.

Entrance: None located.

Floor: Irregular, native clay. Floor rises at north side of room.

Hearth: Sandstone slabs on south and west sides; short fragment on north. Ash from within hearth and adjacent floor areas. Sandstone slabs possibly robbed from hearth in Ruin C, Room 3.

Pit: The hearth, built partly over a subfloor pit indicates remodeling or former occupation.

Postholes: There are three shallow postholes(?); the deepest is 0.18 m.

Material culture on floor: 1 piece of worked hematite, 1 tuff concertion and 1 mano fragment are all from the floor pit.

Phase assignment: Ruin C, Room 1 appears to be a single-roomed structure.

Room 2

Illustrations: Fig. 14.

Shape: Rectangular.

Dimensions: North-south, 6.00 m.(?); east-west, 2.05 m. Depth from surface, 0.15 to 0.45 m.

Construction: The east, south and west walls are a single row of upright, unshaped, tuff boulders. Northern termination of the room is not definitely known.

Entrance: None located.

Floor: Plaster evidence very spotty. Floor on compacted trashy fill, partly overlying Pithouse 7. Floor suffered from rodent activity.

Hearth: In "center" of room. Fire-racked tuff spalls outline the south and part of the east side of the hearth. Ash filled depression to the north of the tuff spalls.

Postholes: Four small, shallow and nebulous postholes are located at the base of the tuff boulders along the east wall.

Material culture on floor: 3 manos and handstones, 2 metates, 2 hammerstones, 1 maul, 1 abrading stone, 2 ceramic tubes.

Phase assignment: Reserve Phase.

Remarks: A contiguous room of similar masonry lies to the south of Room 2, measuring 2.10 by 7.60 m.

In addition there are surface indications for several other narrow, boulder-lined structures around the north end of the site.

Room 3

Illustrations: Figs. 44, 45.

Shape: Square(?).

Dimensions: North-south, 3.65 m.; east-west, 3.55 m.(?). Depth from present surface varies from 0.35 to 0.50 m.

Construction: All walls are set on native clay. The north wall continues as the north wall for Room 1 of Ruin C.

The east wall is indicated by the coping up of floor plaster, but there is no masonry.

The core-and-rubble south wall is 0.35 m. thick. The lower course is large tuff and basalt boulders interspersed with pebbles and cobbles (rubble). Many tuff pebbles in the room fill near the wall indicate that the wall was probably veneered with rubble.

Part of the west wall is overlain by the east wall of Ruin C, Room 1. The lower portion of the wall is large basalt and tuff boulders interspersed with smaller cobbles. It averages 0.40 m.

Fig. 44. Ruin C, Rooms 1 and 3.

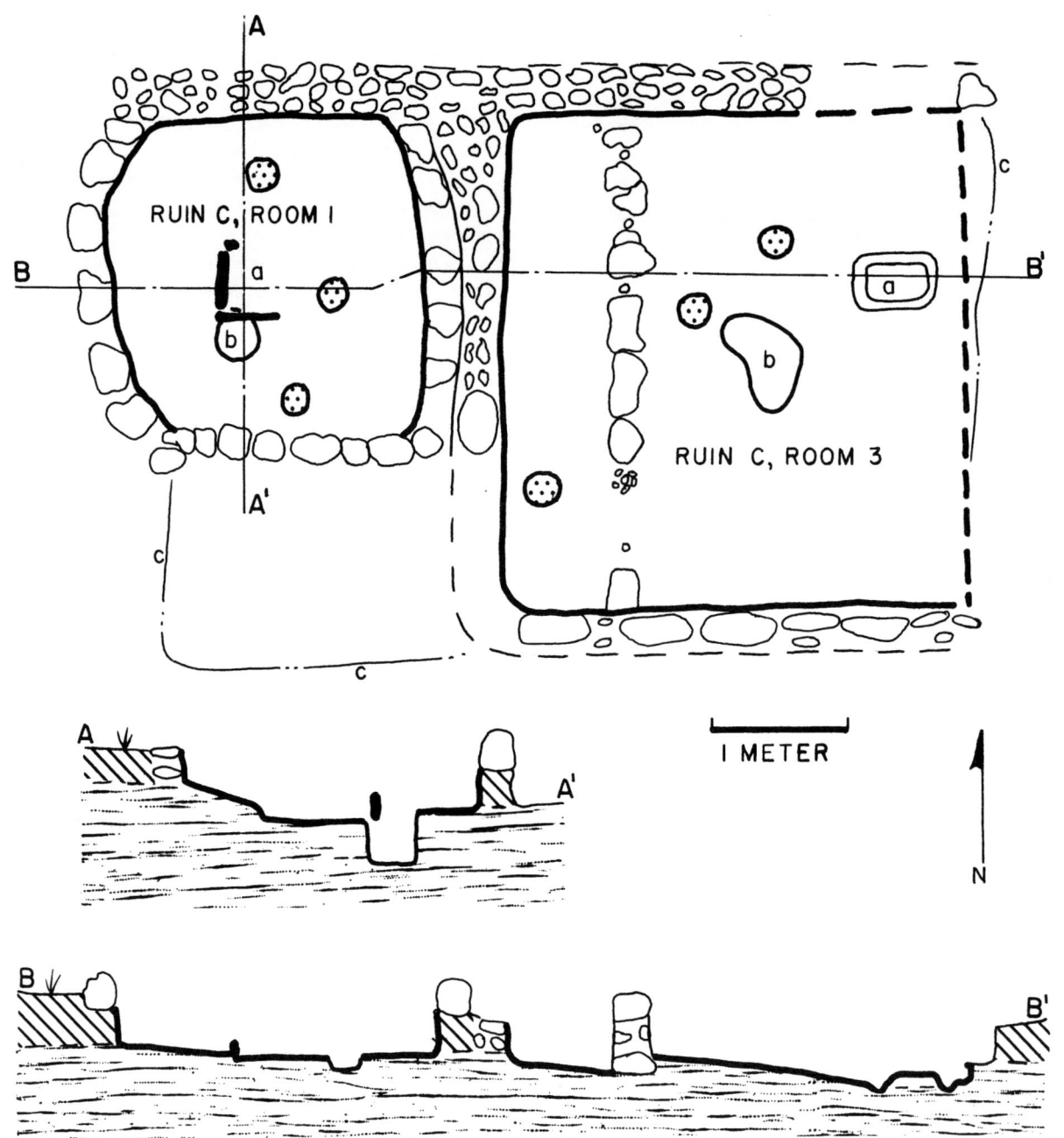

Fig. 45. Plan and sections of Ruin C, Rooms 1 and 3. Horizontal streak, native clay; hatching, trash; stipple, postholes; *a,* hearths; *b,* storage pit; *c,* limit of excavation.

in thickness and was probably faced with rubble.

The partition wall across the western end of the room is 0.25 to 0.30 m. thick and the base rocks are the footing for a jacal upper wall. Within the partition wall base of basalt boulders are five small postholes. The second posthole from the south wall is outlined with pebbles which are set into the floor.

Entrance: None located.

Floor: Irregular, on native clay. Plaster preserved only at wall bases where it copes up onto the lower course of masonry.

Hearth: The hearth is a 0.13 m. thick, highly compacted ashbed near the east side of the room. A groove around the perimeter of the ash area and one sandstone slab fragment indicate that the hearth was originally slab-lined. The sandstone slabs set around the hearth in Ruin C, Room 1 were probably robbed from Room 3.

Pit: A sub-floor pit, 0.40 m. deep, is near the geographic center of the room.

Postholes: In addition to the five small postholes incorporated into the partition wall base there are three other shallow postholes in a diagonal line across the northwest half of the room.

Material culture on floor: 2 manos or handstones, 2 metate fragments, 2 hammerstones, 1 grinding slab, 1 abrading stone, 1 polishing stone.

Phase assignment: Early Tularosa Phase.

Remarks: The partitioning of rooms is a Tularosa Phase trait in the Back River Branch.

DISCUSSION

Ruin B is a discrete architectural unit. The style of masonry is called core-and-rubble. The basal course is shaped tuff and basalt boulders. The second course is a rubble of pebbles and cobbles set in copious amounts of clay. The third course is like the first in the one instance where three courses are found. The walls are faced with a veneer of pebbles, cobbles, and clay mortar. Veneered masonry walls are associated with Tularosa Phase dwellings at Point of Pines. The upper walls of Ruin B were probably jacal.

Each room of Ruin B has a different hearth type. This is a feature at Arizona W: 10: 37, a Tularosa Phase Pueblo at Point of Pines. A definite area for milling activities is found at both Arizona W: 10: 37 and in Ruin B.

Portions of Ruin B, Rooms 1 and 3 overlie Pithouse 4.

The Tularosa Phase is known in the Black River Branch from medium to large size pueblos. However, the presence of nearby agricultural lands accounts for this unit. Ruin B at Nantack Village is a three-room Tularosa Phase unit, probably best classified as an outlying farm settlement.

Ruin C, Room 1 is a later structure than Ruin C, Room 3. Two of the walls are set on approximately 25 cm. of trash and one wall overlies the west wall of Room 3. These three walls, formed of a single row of spaced boulders, are probably the basal supports of a jacal upper wall. Assignment of Ruin C, Room 1 to the late Tularosa Phase is feasible.

Ruin C, Room 3 is older than Ruin C, Room 1. Assignment of this structure to the Tularosa Phase is based on: (1) the south and west walls are a form of the core-and-rubble construction found in Ruin B and, (2) the presence of a partitioning wall.

Ruin C, Room 2 is an elongated rectangle outlined by a single row of upright, tuff boulders. Superposition of part of Ruin C, Room 2 over Pithouse 7, the indeterminate semi-subterranean unit, and the shallowness of the structure account for the vagueness of the interpretation. Architecturally the room is similar to Reserve Phase rooms at Arizona W: 10: 56.

In addition to the definable surface rooms there is other evidence of post-Nantack Phase occupation at Nantack Village.

Pithouse 3. Upslope from Pithouse 3 is a surface unit which could not be defined because two large Ponderosa pines are growing within the rock mound. The three upright slabs which presumably belong to this later unit are shown in Figure 5. The post-1050 pottery in the fill of Pithouse 3 is attributed to this unit(s).

Pithouse 5. Alignments of rock were encountered during excavation in the western half of Pithouse 5. Patches of floor plaster were detected at various levels but it was not possible to correlate these with any of the concentrations of rock. None of the plaster patches or rocks were on the floor of Pithouse 5.

The circuit in the eastern side of Pithouse 5 is the result of subsequent occupation, on the basis of its placement and the presence of McDonald Patterned Corrugated and Mimbres Black-on-white sherds.

Pithouse 6. In the fill of the southeast section of Pithouse 6 was a "corner" formed by upright slabs. The north-south oriented wing of this corner was in line with the "footing trench" shown in Figures 9, 10. There were four tuff boulders in this trench and its placement high on the south wall does not appear to be for ventilation purposes. No footing trench was found in line with the east-west wing of upright slabs. North of the "corner" an ash or hearth area was found 0.25 to 0.50 m. below the surface and at the same level were four metate fragments. It is possible that the semi-circle of postholes around the northern half of Pithouse 6 were associated with this fire area.

It is thought that an elongated, rectangular surface room, similar to the Reserve Phase Ruin C, Room 2, was constructed which partially overlapped the depression formed after the abandonment of Pithouse 6. The absence of more building rock could be the result of robbing for construction of the Tularosa Phase rooms at the site. The upright slabs or corner within the pithouse could be the footing for a wall. The tops of the upright slabs were on approximately the same level as the bottom of the "footing trench" and, as stated, in direct alignment.

Pithouse 10. There was a possible surface structure to the northwest of Pithouse 10. The alignment of large tuff boulders is probably a wall. The break in the northwest wall of Pithouse 10 may indicate a functional connection between the two areas.

Great Kiva. In the northwest corner of the Great Kiva fill was a rock concentration. All the rocks were resting on at least 0.15 m. of trash above the floor. There was a rock alignment on the east side of the shallow trench (Fig. 15). Significance of this trench is not known. The presence of rocks over the large postholes of the Great Kiva and the presence of Burial 2 above the floor indicate that these features were intrusive into the depression of the ceremonial unit after its abandonment.

There is evidence of post-Nantack Phase occupation in the depressions of Pithouse 5, 6, and the Great Kiva. In all cases architectural details are fragmentary and no phase assignments are made.

Areas adjacent to Pithouses 3 and 10 show evidence of post-Nantack surface rooms. They are unexcavated and no phase assignments are made.

POTTERY

The ceramic materials from the surface units are treated in terms of the following categories:

Sherds	3861
Whole or restorable vessels	2
Alma Plain bowl	1
Alma Smudged bowl	1
Sherd discs, perforate	3
Sherd scraper	1
Ceramic pendant, fragment	1
Ceramic tubes	2
Total	3870

Only sherds excavated from within the physical limits of defined rock walls are regarded as belonging to the surface rooms. Summary sherd tabulations are shown in Table 4. Detailed sherd tabulations are available in Breternitz (1956).

The 3861 sherds from all the surface rooms are classified as follows:

	Frequency	Number
Plainware	59.4%	2294
Redware	15.0%	578
Textured pottery	18.9%	730
Painted and intrusive pottery	6.7%	259

TABLE 4. SHERDS FROM SURFACE STRUCTURES

Pottery Type	Ruin B			Ruin C			Total
	Rm. 1	Rm. 2	Rm. 3	Rm. 1	Rm. 2	Rm. 3	
Plain, Red, and Textured Types							
Alma Plain	178	41	107	199	1224	399	2148
Alma Smudged	6	7	7	12	57	19	108
Alma Polished					9	11	20
Alma Scored			3	1	2	4	10
Alma Incised			1			1	2
Alma Punched		4	2				6
Redware Jars	7	1	11	41	109	81	250
Redware Bowls	23	4	13	29	176	57	302
Redware Smudged		3		3	10	9	25
San Francisco Red, Coiled Exterior	1						1
Alma Neck Banded	3						3
Three Circle Neck Corrugated				2	6	6	14
Pine Flat Neck Corrugated	2			18	69	22	111
Reserve Incised Corrugated				2	6		8
Reserve Punched Corrugated					1		1
Reserve Plain Corrugated	14	8	5	17	18	36	98
Reserve Indented Corrugated	46	51	77	22	62	41	299
Red Slipped Corrugated				3	3	11	17
Tularosa Patterned Corrugated	19	2	24			7	52
Point of Pines Obliterated Corrugated	15	3	19	2	13	22	74
Tularosa Fillet Rim	7	2	7			3	19
McDonald Painted Corrugated						1	1
McDonald Patterned Corrugated	8		10	3		11	32
McDonald Grooved Corrugated						1	1
Sub-total	329	126	286	354	1765	742	3602
Painted and Intrusive Types							
Encinas Red-on-brown				10	75	20	105
Nantack Red-on-brown				1	1		2
Sacaton Red-on-buff					2		2
Sacaton Red-on-buff, Safford Variety				2	3	7	12
Buff Ware, Safford Region					3		3
Gila Plain					3		3
Wingate Black-on-red			1	1			2
Pinedale Black-on-red				1		2	3
Maverick Mountain Black-on-red						1	1
White Mountain Red Ware						1	1
Unknown Black-on-red						1	1
Mangus Black-on-white					17	16	33
Mimbres Black-on-white				3	25	13	41
Mimbres White Wares				1	9	6	16
Gray Wares						2	2
Red Mesa Black-on-white				1			1
Snowflake Black-on-white				1	1		2
PII Glaze Black-on-white					1		1
Reserve Black-on-white	1			4	4	2	11
Tularosa Black-on-white		2					2
Unknown Northern Black-on-white	1	1		3	2	1	8
Northern White Wares	3		1				4
St. Johns Polychrome						1	1
Pinedale Polychrome		1					1
Pinto Polychrome				1			1
Sub-total	5	4	2	29	146	73	259
TOTAL	334	130	288	383	1911	815	3861

PLAINWARE

Alma Plain, Point of Pines Variety. This is the dominant pottery type for all the surface units. The one whole vessel (Fig. 46 a) does not provide information on shape changes.

Alma Smudged. Sherds of smudged plainware are not distinguishable from the Alma Smudged found in the pithouses. Smudged plainware found in similar time horizons in the Reserve Region is called Reserve Smudged.

An eroded, Alma Smudged bowl is shown in Figure 46 b.

Alma Polished. Less than 1% of all sherds are polished brownware.

Alma Scored, Alma Incised, and Alma Punched. These persist as minor types in the surface rooms.

REDWARE

San Francisco Red, Point of Pines Variety and Reserve Red, Point of Pines Variety. Both redware types are recognized from the surface rooms. Field observations and laboratory reanalysis indicate that the proportion of Reserve Red to San Francisco Red is higher in the surface rooms than in the Nantack Phase pithouses.

TEXTURED POTTERY

Alma Neck Banded. The three sherds are from the room fill of Ruin B, Room 1.

Three Circle Neck Corrugated. The 14 sherds generally occur high in room fill.

Pine Flat Neck Corrugated. The 111 sherds indicate that this type continues at least into the Reserve Phase. No information is available on vessel shape change.

Reserve Incised Corrugated and Reserve Punched Corrugated. These occur as minor types in the room fill of Ruin C, Rooms 1 and 2.

Reserve Plain Corrugated. This type is found in every surface room.

Reserve Indented Corrugated. This is the most numerous textured type from all of the surface rooms. It emphasizes the time differential between pithouse and surface units. Neck corrugation is typical of the Nantack Phase units and all-over corrugation is typical for the surface rooms.

Red Slipped Corrugated, Tularosa Patterned Corrugated, Point of Pines Obliterated Corrugated, and Tularosa Fillet Rim. Each type is present in a much greater relative frequency in the surface rooms than in the pithouses.

McDonald Painted Corrugated, McDonald Patterned Corrugated, and McDonald Grooved Corrugated. The higher proportion of McDonald Patterned Corrugated to McDonald Painted Corrugated is a time differential indicator when compared with the relative occurrence of these types from the pithouses.

PAINTED AND INTRUSIVE POTTERY

Encinas Red-on-brown. This is still the most popular decorated type during the occupation of the surface rooms. At Point of Pines Encinas Red-on-brown is found in significant amounts through the Tularosa Phase.

Nantack Red-on-brown. Ruin C, Rooms 1 and 2 each have one sherd in the room fill.

Sacaton Red-on-buff and Sacaton Red-on-buff, Safford Variety. The 14 sherds of these Hohokam types are all from room fill.

Buff Ware, Safford Region and Gila Plain. Three sherds each of these types are from the room fill of Ruin C, Room 3.

Wingate Black-on-red. This type is represented by two sherds. However, the sherd from the floor of Ruin B, Room 3 is classified as Wingate Black-on-red only after consultation with four colleagues. Two archaeologists agree with the author that the sherd is Wingate Black-on-red and two express the opinion that it might better be classified as Pinedale Black-on-red.

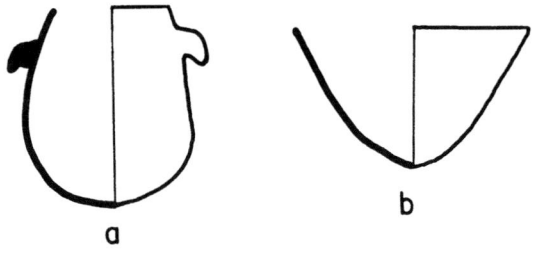

FIG. 46. Vessel shapes of plainware. *a*, Alma Plain bowl; *b*, Alma Smudged bowl. Height of *a*, 10.2 cm.

Pinedale Black-on-red (Colton and Hargrave 1937: 106). The three sherds are from the fill of Ruin C, Rooms 1 and 3.

Maverick Mountain Black-on-red (Colton 1955a: 8). This beveled rim bowl sherd is a type associated with the late Tularosa Phase and the Maverick Mountain Phase at Point of Pines.

Unknown Black-on-red and White Mountain Redware. One sherd of each type is in the fill of Ruin C, Room 3.

Mangas Black-on-white. The 33 sherds of this type are found in Ruin C, Rooms 2 and 3.

Mimbres Black-on-white. Preponderance of Mimbres Black-on-white over Mangas Black-on-white again denotes a time difference in the occupation of surface and pithouse units.

Mimbres White Ware and Gray Wares. These categories designate intrusive wares. Neither classification includes painted sherds.

Red Mesa, Snowflake, and Pueblo II Glaze Black-on-whites. These types are represented by one, two, and one sherds respectively.

Reserve Black-on-white. This type is relatively more abundant than in the pithouse units.

Tularosa Black-on-white. The two sherds, both from the fill of Ruin B, Room 1, are indicators of the Tularosa Phase in the Black River Branch.

Unknown Northern Black-on-whites and Northern White Wares. These two categories include unidentifiable black-on-whites and undecorated white wares of northern origin.

St. Johns Polychrome (Martin, Rinaldo and Bluhm 1954: 73). This sherd, from Ruin C, Room 3, is the glaze paint variety of St. Johns Polychrome.

Pinedale Polychrome (Colton and Hargrave 1937: 107). The large rim sherd of Pinedale Polychrome, with color and exterior treatment overtones of Springerville Polychrome, is from Ruin B, Room 2.

Pinto Polychrome (Colton and Hargrave 1937: 87). A classic example of Pinto Polychrome is in the fill of Ruin C, Room 1.

WHOLE VESSELS

The two whole or restorable vessels from the surface rooms are the following types:

Alma Plain bowl (Fig. 46 *a*) 1
Alma Smudged bowl (Fig. 46 *b*) 1

The Alma Plain bowl is from the floor of Ruin B, Room 3 and the Alma Smudged bowl from the fill of Ruin B, Room 3.

MISCELLANEOUS POTTERY OBJECTS

Sherd Discs, Perforate. All three specimens have biconical perforations; two with well-ground edges; one with edges slightly ground.

Material: Redware jars (2), Redware bowls, smudged (1).

Provenience: Floor, Ruin B, Room 2 (1), Room 3 (2).

Sherd Scraper. One specimen; oval, redware jar sherd with one end used for scraping.

Provenience: Room fill, Ruin B, Room 1 (1).

Ceramic Pendant, Fragment. One fragment of purposefully made brownware disc; surface polished; cylindrical perforation.

Provenience: Room fill, Ruin B, Room 1 (1).

Ceramic Tubes (Fig. 47). Two specimens; Alma Plain, Point of Pines Variety paste; cucumber-shaped tubes with longitudinal perforations. The thick-walled specimen was made by perforating the roughly modeled clay with a cylindrical object. Dimensions: length, 204 mm.; maximum diameter, 55 mm.; thickness, 10 mm.; diameter of openings, 10 and 11 mm. The thin-walled ceramic tube was made by the coil and scrape method. Dimensions: length, 192 mm.; maximum diameter, 47 mm.; thickness, 5 mm.;

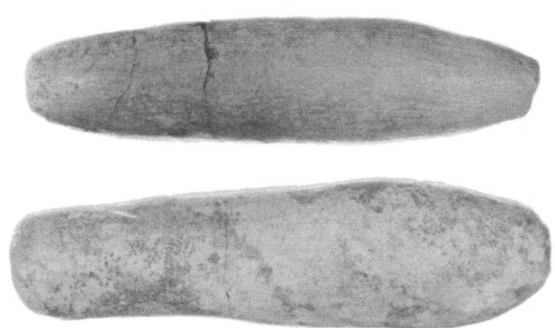

FIG. 47. Brownware ceramic tubes.

diameter of openings, 13 and 15 mm.

Provenience: Floor, Ruin C, Room 2 (2).

Discussion

Detailed sherd tabulations for the surface rooms excavated at Nantack Village are on file at the Library, University of Arizona (Breternitz 1956).

Although a similarity does exist between the pottery from the surface rooms and the pithouses at Nantack Village there is a definite difference in the popularity of certain types.

Eighteen pottery types from the pithouse excavations are lacking from the inventory of types for the surface units. These are: Alma Rough; Alma Grooved; San Francisco Red, Punched Exterior; Reserve Fillet Rim; Prieto Indented Corrugated; Point of Pines Punctate; Santa Cruz Red-on-buff; Buff Ware, Gila Basin; Showlow Black-on-red; Puerco Black-on-red; Deadmans Black-on-gray; Kiatuthlanna Black-on-white; Corduroy Black-on-white; Holbrook Black-on-white; Puerco Black-on-white; Whipple Black-on-white; Little Colorado Corrugated; Maverick Mountain Polychrome.

Four decorated types are found in the surface rooms that are not in the Nantack Phase features. There are: Pinedale Black-on-red; Maverick Mountain Black-on-red; Pinedale Polychrome; Pinto Polychrome.

All-over corrugation is typical for textured pottery from the surface rooms; neck corrugation is typical for the Nantack Phase.

The scarcity of datable pottery types in association with floor features of surface rooms makes phase assignment insecure. However, the ceramic evidence corroborates the data derived from architectural information for the six excavated surface units.

The three rooms of Ruin B are Tularosa Phase and better dated by ceramics than the other surface rooms at the site.

Ruin C, Room 3 is also Tularosa Phase. This room is earlier in the phase than Ruin C, Room 1 which is placed in the late Tularosa Phase.

Ruin C, Room 2 is Reserve Phase.

The two ceramic tubes are from the floor of Ruin C, Room 2. A noise similar to the sound produced by blowing across the mouth of a soda pop bottle can be made with the tubes, by closing one end and blowing across the open end. These objects are possibly noise makers or sucking tubes. There is no evidence that they were used as pipes.

ARTIFACTS

Stone, bone, and shell artifacts from the six excavated surface rooms are tabulated on the basis of descriptions already given for similar artifacts from the Nantack Phase occupation. Variations within types are recognized and distinct types are formulated for artifacts which do not fit the established categories.

Ground Stone

Ground stone tools from the surface rooms are classified as follows:

	Individual Types	Total
Metates		2
Type 2, basin	1	
Type 3a, closed-end trough or "scoop"	1	
Grinding slabs		2
Type 1a, uniface, unshaped	2	
Manos		5
Type 1a, uniface, round to oval	3	
Type 1b, uniface, retangular	2	
Handstones		4
Type 1, uniface	2	
Type 2, biface	2	
Polishing stones		3
Type 1, pebble	3	
Abrading stones		2
Type 1, uniface	2	
Grooved abrading stone		1
Hammerstones		14
Type 1, spherical to angular	12	
Type 2, pitted	1	
Grooved maul		1
Total		33

METATES

Type 2, Basin. One specimen; grinding surface shallow, unshaped boulder.
> Material: Light, fine-grained igneous rock (1).
> Provenience: Room fill, Ruin C, Room 3 (1).

Type 3a, Closed-end trough or scoop. One specimen.
> Material: Porphyritic basalt (1).
> Provenience: Floor, Ruin B, Room 2 (1).

GRINDING SLABS

Type 1a, Uniface, unshaped. Two specimens. Sandstone slab from Ruin B, Room 2 in front of sherd plastered into floor; possibly grinding bin. Other specimen has slightly basin-shaped grinding depression.
> Material: Sandstone (1), tuff (1).
> Provenience: Floor, Ruin B, Room 2 (1), Ruin C, Room 3 (1).

MANOS

Type 1a, Uniface, round to oval. All three specimens have edges shaped by pecking.
> Material: Vesicular basalt (2), fine-grained basalt (1).
> Provenience: Room fill, Ruin B, Room 1 (1), Ruin C, Rooms 2 (1), 3 (1).

Type 1b, Uniface, rectangular. Two specimens; one with pecked finger grooves.
> Material: Vesicular basalt (2).
> Provenience: Floor, Ruin C, Room 2 (2).

HANDSTONES

Type 1, Uniface. Two specimens, one with all edges shaped; other with one edge shaped.
> Material: Fine-grained basalt (1), tuff (1).
> Provenience: Room fill, Ruin C, Room 3 (2).

Type 2, Biface. Two specimens; one broken specimen is re-used as a hammerstone.
> Material: Sandstone (1), vesicular basalt (1).
> Provenience: Room fill, Ruin C, Rooms 2 (1), 3 (1).

POLISHING STONES

Type 1, Pebble. Three specimens; longest specimen has transverse polishing marks; limestone unusual material for polishing stone.
> Material: Fine-grained basalts (2), limestone (1).
> Provenience: Floor, Ruin C, Room 3 (1); Floor fill, Ruin B, Room 3 (1); Backdirt, Ruin C, Room 2 (1).

ABRADING STONES

Type 1, Uniface. Two specimens, one made from percussion flaked tuff cobble; other has shallow, grooved abrading surface, little used.
> Material: Sandstone (1), tuff (1).
> Provenience: Floor, Ruin C, Rooms 2 (1), 3 (1).

GROOVED ABRADING STONE

One specimen; roughly rectangular; all surfaces polished except broken end; longitudinal groove well-polished; opposite surface has slightly concave grinding facet with remnants of red paint.
> Material: Limestone (1).
> Provenience: Floor, Ruin B, Room 3 (1).

HAMMERSTONES

Type 1, Spherical to angular. Twelve specimens; one has a partially ground face; one has three polishing facets.
> Material: Quartz (4), fine-grained basalt (3), tuff (2), vesicular basalt (1), rhyolite (1), chert (1).
> Provenience: Floor, Ruin C, Rooms 2 (1), 3 (2); Floor fill, Ruin B, Rooms 3 (1); Room fill, Ruin C, Rooms 1 (1), 2 (1), 3 (6).

Type 2, Pitted. One specimen; artifact type not recognized in Nantack Phase material. Discoidal shaped; battering evident around greatest circumference; differs from Type 1 hammerstone by having two shallow, pecked finger grips on flat sides; small rubbed facet on one side.
> Material: Fine-grained basalt (1).
> Provenience: Room fill, Ruin C, Room 2 (1).

GROOVED MAUL

One specimen; probably seven-eighths or full-grooved; groove distinct on only half of maul; groove centered on maul; ends almost flat with rounded edges; small rubbed facet on each side suggests specimen is a re-used mano.
> Material: Fine-grained basalt (1).
> Provenience: Floor, Ruin C, Room 2 (1).

MINERALS AND CURIOS

Hematite. Two specimens from Ruin C, Room 1. One, from small floor pit, very dense with three rubbed facets and two rubbed grooves on one side.

Quartz Crystal. Ruin C, fill, Room 3 (1).

Tuff Geodes. Floor pit, Ruin C, Room 1 (1); Room fill, Ruin C, Room 3 (1).

Flaked Stone

Flaked stone tools from the surface rooms are classified as follows:

	Individual Types	Total
Projectile Points		2
Stemmed		
Type 3, diagonal notches, straight stem, small	1	
Side Notched		
Type 6, shallow side notches	1	
Knives		2
Type 1, flake knives	2	
Type 3, humpbacked, small	2	
Blades-Saws		3
Total		12

Projectile Points

Projectile point types are described in the Flaked Stone Artifact section of the Nantack Phase Occupation chapter.

Type 3, Stemmed. Diagonal notches, straight stem, small. One specimen.

Material: Obsidian (1).
Provenience: Room fill, Ruin C, Room 1.

Type 6, Side Notched. Shallow side notches. One specimen.

Material: Obsidian (1).
Provenience: Room fill, Ruin C, Room 3 (1).

Knives

Type 1, Flake knives. Two specimens.
Material: Chert (2).
Provenience: Room fill, Ruin C, Room 1 (2).

Scrapers

Type 2, Side. Three specimens.
Material: Chert (1), rhyolite (1), igneous (1).
Provenience: Room fill, Ruin C, Rooms 1 (1), 3 (2).

Type 3, Humpbacked, small. Two specimens; artifact type not recognized in Nantack Phase material. Small random flakes with retouching on less than one-quarter of one corner; high angle scraping edge, over 45 degrees.

Material: Chert (2).
Provenience: Room fill, Ruin C, Rooms 1 (1), 2 (1).

Blades-Saws

All three specimens single edged; two with straight and one with convex cutting edge.

Material: Flow basalt (3).
Provenience: Floor, Ruin B, Room 3 (1); Room fill, Ruin B, Rooms 1 (1), 3 (1).

Bone

The distal portion of a splinter bone awl is the only bone artifact from the surface rooms at Nantack Village.

Discussion

The small number of complete stone tools from the surface rooms does not permit generalizations on changes in artifact types for the different occupations of Nantack Village. However, the five manos are all uniface.

There are two stone tools from the surface rooms that are lacking from the Nantack Phase pithouses. One is a specialized hammerstone with shallow, pecked finger grips on the flat sides of the battering instrument. The other is a small, humpbacked, high angle scraper.

Generally speaking the stone tools from the surface rooms are continuations of types described for the Nantack Phase. An architectural-lithic innovation in the surface rooms is the presence of milling areas in Ruin B.

SUMMARY

Architecture and associated sherd material show that the six excavated surface rooms at Nantack Village are Reserve and Tularosa phase habitations. The presence of nearby agricultural lands and the physical separation of the architectural units probably indicates that Nantack Village was the site of outlying farm houses during the A.D. 1000-1275 period.

Only material recovered from within the limits of defined surface rooms is assigned to the Reserve and Tularosa Phases. The ceramic material is mixed with the previous Nantack Phase occupation but the relative abundance of certain pottery types and the presence of post-Nantack Phase types show that the surface dwellings were all occupied after A.D. 1000.

4

BURIALS

THERE are four human burials from Nantack Village. The characteristics of each are:

Burial 1

Sex: Male.

Age: Adult, over 50 years old.

Nature of grave: Shallow sub-surface burial into black, silty trash between Pithouses 3 and 5. Mixed native and native clays below skeleton undisturbed. Base of skull only 25 cm. below the surface.

Position: Indeterminate due to absence of lower portion of body.

Orientation: Head toward southeast.

Deformation: Occipital.

Grave furniture: There is a high percentage of corrugated pottery in the 145 sherds from the burial excavation. One side scraper was excavated with Burial 1.

Dating: On the basis of the pottery from the burial excavation and the occipital deformation Burial 1 belongs to the post-Nantack Phase occupation of the site.

Burial 2

Sex: Indeterminate.

Age: 7-8 years.

Nature of grave: Bones in fill above a main support posthole in the northwest corner of the Great Kiva and associated with, and under, the northern portion of the fill rock concentration. Part of the skeleton was recovered in 1954 and the remainder excavated in 1955.

Position: Extended(?).

Orientation: Skull towards northwest, possibly facing down.

Grave furniture: Miniature Encinas Red-on-brown ladle, miniature Three Circle Neck Corrugated jar, miniature redware jar, miniature plainware jar, and miniature plainware seed jar grouped northeast of the head; shell bracelet above chest; two red stone beads and piece of copper ore(?) between skull and trunk; position of miniature plainware ladle unknown.

Dating: Burial 2 is obviously younger than the Great Kiva due to its superposition over one of the main support postholes. The accompanying Three Circle Neck Corrugated jar and the Encinas Red-on-brown ladle suggest a late Nantack Phase date.

Burial 3

Sex: Male.

Age: Adult, over 50 years old.

Nature of grave: In sheet trash west of Pithouse 9 and the large trash mound. No evidence of burial pit dug into native clay.

Position: Extended, on back. Left leg crossed over right leg at ankle.

Orientation: Skull towards magnetic north; face up.

Deformation: Occipital; cephalic index 103.4.

Reconstructed stature: 160.9 ± 2.5 cm. or $63 \frac{3}{8} \pm 1$ inches. Reconstructed stature based on Stevenson's formulae for North Chinese, with adjusted cadaver height (Hrdlicka 1952: 221).

Grave furniture: A large corrugated sherd

under the right shoulder is the only object in direct association.

Dating: Probably belongs to the post-Nantack Phase, on the basis of the occipital deformation.

Burial 4

Sex: Indeterminate.

Age: Adult.

Nature of grave: Circular pit, 60 cm. in diameter, in bottom of floor pit in northeast corner of Great Kiva.

Position: Flexed.

Orientation: Indeterminate.

Deformation: Indeterminate.

Grave furniture: Alma Smudged bowl in fill of pit above the majority of scattered bones.

Dating: On the basis of the intrusive pit into the larger floor pit a post-Nantack Phase date is probable.

Summary

None of the four burials can be accurately dated. However, the two burials intrusive into the Great Kiva are obviously younger than the Nantack Phase ceremonial unit.

Only the child burial into the fill of the Great Kiva, Burial 2, can be assigned to the Nantack Phase, and this is late in the phase. The practice of occipital deformation in the two instances where cranial shape is determined places both Burial 1 and 3 more logically as younger than the Nantack Phase. Interment of Burials 1 and 3 into thin sheet trash with a mixture of Nantack Phase and later pottery is not conclusive dating evidence.

The interment of Burials 2 and 4 in the Great Kiva fill indicate that these deaths occurred after the ceremonial structure had fallen into disuse. The partially recurved bowl found with Burial 4 has a shape generally associated with post-Nantack phases in the Point of Pines region.

An unassociated mandible was found in the 25 to 50 cm. level of Pithouse 6 and another came from the fill of the large oblong posthole at the entrance of the Great Kiva.

The paucity of burials is a characteristic of Mogollon sites (Wheat 1954: 77). However, there is no evidence of cremation at Nantack Village.

5

CONCLUSIONS

DATING

THIS SECTION is a summary of the dating discussions that follow the descriptive portions of the architecture and ceramics sections for both the Nantack Phase and the later occupation.

The Nantack Phase is assigned to the A.D. 900–1000 period (Fig. 48). There is no dendrochronological material to support this placement. The beginning and ending dates for the Nantack Phase are based on comparisons of material culture, especially ceramics, from adjacent regions. However, with the data available it is impossible to assign the pithouse occupation of Nantack Village to any period other than Mogollon 4, as defined by Wheat (1955).

The Nantack Phase is a pithouse dwelling period in Point of Pines prehistory. Surface dwelling units begin in the Reserve Phase, at about A.D. 1000. Recessed postholes and the occasional use of peripheral boulders, which suggest basal supports for jacal upper walls, are transitional traits from semi-subterranean to surface dwellings. In general, architectural features resemble the Three Circle Phase in the Mimbres and Reserve regions.

The rectangular Great Kiva is the largest Mogollon ceremonial structure which has been completely excavated. Size is the primary criterion for attributing ceremonial or community construction and use. The Great Kiva is characterized by large postholes whose arrangement indicates an asymmetrical roofing arrangement. Kiva floor features are notably lacking. The wide, stepped, eastern entrance is similar to large ceremonial structures in the Forestdale Valley which date after A.D. 1000.

Much of the evidence for dating the Nantack Phase is the presence or absence of certain pottery types. The context of the sherds is of primary importance due to the presence of post-Nantack occupation at Nantack Village (Table 5).

The pottery types present justify the A.D. 900 beginning date for the Nantack Phase as follows: pre-Nantack types occur, but are not abundant. Kiatuthlanna and Corduroy black-on-white sherds are too few in number to be significant. There is no Mogollon Red-on-brown or Three Circle Red-on-white from the site. Three Circle Neck Corrugated and Mangas Black-on-white, both diagnostic types for the Nantack Phase, are associated with the Three Circle Phase in the Mimbres and Reserve regions.

More tenuous than the beginning date of the Nantack Phase is the terminal date. Certain pottery types such as Point of Pines Punctate, the McDonald corrugateds, Tularosa Fillet Rim, Tularosa Black-on-white and numerous black-on-reds occur in quantities too small to extend the end date past A.D. 1000, using the currently accepted ceramic dates for these types.

Reserve Indented Corrugated begins earlier in the Black River Branch than in the Reserve region. Its abundance, plus such types as Pine Flat

Neck Corrugated, textured redwares, and a variety of texturing techniques on the Alma Textured Series, are forerunners to the elaborate surface manipulation which is characteristic of post-Reserve phases at Point of Pines.

A few trade artifacts of stone and shell are useful for dating purposes. The palette fragments, three-quarter grooved axes and shell bracelets are executed in the style associated with the Sacaton Phase at Snaketown. Otherwise, artifacts of stone, bone and antler appear to be indigenous products which compare favorably to similar objects found in adjacent regions on a contemporary time horizon.

The six surface rooms at Nantack Village are assigned to the Reserve and Tularosa phases. Dating rests on an admittedly small amount of evidence and it will be refuted or substantiated when criteria for these periods in the Black River Branch are formalized.

The Chronological "Gap"

As seen in Figure 48, the current conception of phase development and dating at Point of Pines, there is a 300 year gap, plus or minus, between the end of the Circle Prairie Phase and the beginning of the Nantack Phase. On the basis of data available since the publication of Wheat's papers (1954, 1955) I believe the "gap" should be shortened to about 100 years, or entirely closed.

There are no tree-ring dates from Crooked Ridge Village and consequently intrusive ceramics

TABLE 5. POTTERY CROSS-DATING FOR MOGOLLON 4 PHASES*

	Phase			
Pottery Type	Nantack	Three Circle	Cerros	Encinas
San Francisco Red	U	U	U	U
Alma Plain	U	U	U	U
Alma Textured Series	U	U		
Neck Corrugated	U	U	D	D‡
Smudged Brownware	U	U		
Reserve Indented Corrugated	U			
Mogollon Red-on-brown			D	
Three Circle Red-on-white		T	D	
Mangas Black-on-white	T	U		D
Mimbres Black-on-white	S			D
Reserve Black-on-white	S	A		
Gila Plain	S			
Sacaton Red-on-buff	T		D	D‡
Encinas Red-on-brown	U			U
Kiatuthlanna Black-on-white	L	B		
White Mound Black-on-white		B		
Red Mesa Black-on-white	S	C		
Puerco Black-on-white	L			

*	Modified after Wheat 1955, Table 18
‡	Numerically more abundant in Encinas than in Cerro Phase
A	Haury 1936b: 66; Nesbitt 1938: 81
B	Martin and others 1952: 67
C	Haury 1936b: 66
D	Sayles 1945: 47
L	Little of type found at Nantack Village
S	Some of type found at Nantack Village
T	Diagnostic decorated type for phase
U	Resident type, decorated and undecorated

CONCLUSIONS

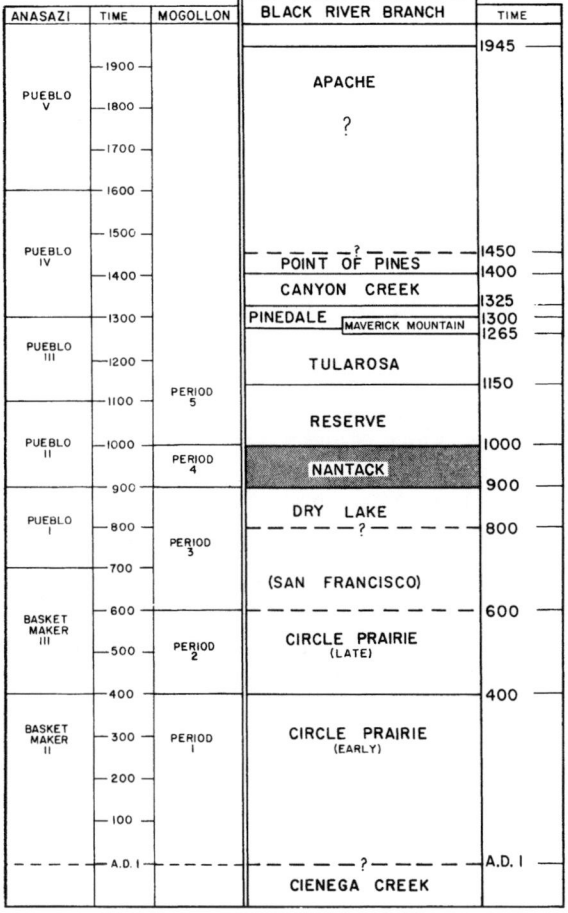

FIG. 48. Phase sequence.

are the primary dating tool. Of the "datable" sherds much reliance is necessarily placed on Hohokam red-on-buff pottery. I do not wish to take issue with the Hohokam chronology used by Wheat but do want to mention the possibility that the occupation of Crooked Ridge Village lasted until at least 800.

The early portion of Crooked Ridge Village is to the north and the later habitations tend to be upridge, or south (Wheat 1954, Fig. 2). Wheat's objective in excavating was to define the early occupation and there are pithouse depressions at the south end of the site which are unexcavated. The possibility that Pithouses 21 and 23 equate with the Three Circle or Nantack and San Francisco phases respectively is mentioned by Wheat (1954: 172). I believe Pithouse 22 is also a dwelling used around A.D. 800. In addition, Pithouse 2 has architectural innovations and only one "datable" sherd, Three Circle Red-on-white, which could make it contemporaneous with Pithouses 21, 22, and 23.

Architecturally and ceramically, Pithouses 2, 21, 22, and 23 at Crooked Ridge Village have the following relationships with the Nantack Phase:

Pithouse 2 (Wheat 1954: 19–22). The overall shape, and the placement of the six postholes fit the definition of Nantack Phase pithouses. However, a northern "annex" is associated which is not known for the Nantack Phase. A Hohokam Pioneer Period ¾ groove axe was on the floor. Pithouse 2 is the earliest of the four pithouses under discussion and the picking apart of separate traits is at best a spurious undertaking.

Pithouse 21 (Wheat 1954: 54–8). Wheat places little faith in the dating of this pithouse due to the ceramic mixture and architectural overlapping but does tentatively place it in the Nantack Phase, formerly called Three Circle Phase (Wheat 1954: 179).

Pithouse 22 (Wheat 1954: 38–9, 41). The posthole pattern of this pithouse is strikingly similar to Pithouses 1, 3 and 6 at Nantack Village. The lack of datable intrusives does not eliminate the possibility that Pithouse 22 was occupied as late as the 10th century.

Pithouse 23 (Wheat 1954: 39, 41). I believe Wheat is justified in assigning this pithouse to the San Francisco Phase time period, A.D. 600–800.

Chronological "gaps" in regions of favorable environment for aboriginal living are difficult to explain. Unless there was a striking local climatic change at Point of Pines there should be sites which belong to the A.D. 600–800 period. With this implication and the "feeling" that no chronological gap exists, I propose the "gap" be narrowed from A.D. 600–900 to 800–900, with the distinct possibility that there is no gap. The only void in our present knowledge of Point of Pines prehistory is probably due to the insufficient sampling of the pertinent time periods.

COMMUNITY PATTERN

The dearth of information available on prehistoric Southwestern settlement patterns has been formalized by Haury (1956). Attempts to fit Southwestern archaeological data into worldwide, systematic categories of community patterning have also met with limited success (Meggers 1956).

However, certain implications on settlement pattern during the A.D. 900–1000 period in the Black River Branch are worthy of mention. The following comments are based on the architectural data for the Nantack Phase and excavation notes on Arizona W: 10: 79, a Nantack Phase site near Point of Pines partially excavated in 1953.

Arizona W: 10: 79 is similar to Nantack Village in the following traits: (1) ceramic complex fits very neatly that defined for the Nantack Phase, (2) nearby agricultural lands, (3) located on a minor ridge at the edge of Circle Prairie, (4) pithouses apparently placed without pattern, (5) at least two of the six excavated pithouses are "good" Nantack Phase units, (6) Reserve Phase surface structures indicate continued use of the site and account for some of the ceramic mixture.

There is no ceremonial structure at Arizona W: 10: 79 and it is a smaller site than Nantack Village. There is, in addition, no evidence from the extensive survey of the Point of Pines region of any Nantack Phase sites, other than Nantack Village, with Great Kivas. The implication is that Nantack Village served as the county seat of spiritual endeavor within the A.D. 900–1000 period. Thus, the site is not the typical small village of the Nantack Phase and may have features, typical or atypical, that would not be repeated in extensive excavations at other Nantack Phase sites. However, the range of material culture evidence from Nantack Village will make it possible to designate Nantack Phase sites, if and when excavated, primarily on the basis of ceramics.

It is entirely possible that there was a similar ceremonial site in the earlier Circle Prairie Phase. Crooked Ridge Village has at least two Great Kivas (Wheat 1954: 58–64). There are other sites dating in the Circle Prairie Phase in the Point of Pines region, but I do not know of any that have Great Kivas. Thus, Crooked Ridge Village might be the ceremonial site or center of the Circle Prairie Phase. If this situation, for both the Circle Prairie and Nantack Phases, could be demonstrated as fact it would resemble the nuclear pattern of sites and ceremonial centers presented for the Viru Valley of Peru (Willey 1953).

Using the foregoing as a working hypothesis we may apply currently accepted terms to describe the situation. Considered separately Nantack Village and Arizona W: 10: 79 are "communities" (Meggers 1956: 133). If a ceremonial relationship exists they may be classed together as a "community pattern" verging on "Simple Nuclear Centered" (Meggers 1956: 134, 141–3).

SUMMARY

At Nantack Village, an archaeological site near Point of Pines, Arizona, 11 semi-subterranean pithouses, including a Great Kiva, were excavated. From the analysis of the material culture the Nantack Phase of the Black River Branch of the Mogollon Culture has been defined. This A.D. 900 to 1000 phase is characterized by rectangular, semi-subterranean pithouses and a large rectangular Great Kiva. Pottery is the major criterion for determining the date of pithouse occupation. Plainware, redware, and textured wares are the local ceramic products. Decorated pottery types were obtained from the north, east and south, but some red-on-brown pottery was made in the Point of Pines locality.

Six surface rooms occupied during the Reserve and Tularosa phases were also excavated and have been briefly described.

REFERENCES

BAILEY, VERNON
1931 Mammals of New Mexico. *U.S. Department of Agriculture, Bureau of Biological Survey, North American Fauna,* No. 53. Washington.

BRETERNITZ, D. A.
1956 The Archaeology of Nantack Village, Point of Pines, Arizona. MS, master's thesis, University of Arizona, Tucson.

COLTON, H. S.
1941 Winona and Ridge Ruin, Part II. *Museum of Northern Arizona, Bulletin,* No. 19. Flagstaff.

1955a Check List of Southwestern Pottery Types. *Museum of Northern Arizona, Ceramic Series,* No. 2. Flagstaff.

1955b Pottery Types of the Southwest. *Museum of Northern Arizona, Ceramic Series,* No. 3a. Flagstaff.

COLTON, H. S. AND L. L. HARGRAVE
1937 Handbook of Northern Arizona Pottery Wares. *Museum of Northern Arizona, Bulletin,* No. 11. Flagstaff.

COSGROVE, H. S. AND C. B. COSGROVE
1932 The Swarts Ruin, a Typical Mimbres Site in Southwestern New Mexico. *Papers of the Peabody Museum, Harvard University,* Vol. 15. Cambridge.

DANSON, E. B.
1957 An Archaeological Survey of West-Central New Mexico and East-Central Arizona. *Papers of the Peabody Museum, Harvard University,* Vol. 44, No. 1. Cambridge.

GIFFORD, J. C.
1957 Archaeological Explorations in Caves of the Point of Pines Region. MS, master's thesis, University of Arizona, Tucson.

GIFFORD, J. C. (EDITOR)
1956 *A Guide to the Description of Pottery Types in the Southwest,* revised. Department of Anthropology, University of Arizona, Tucson.

GLADWIN, H. S.
- 1945 The Chaco Branch: Excavations at White Mound and in the Red Mesa Valley. *Medallion Papers,* No. 33. Gila Pueblo, Globe.
- 1948 Excavations at Snaketown, IV: Review and Conclusions. *Medallion Papers,* No. 38. Gila Pueblo, Globe.

GLADWIN, H. S., E. W. HAURY, E. B. SAYLES, AND NORA GLADWIN
- 1937 Excavations at Snaketown: Material Culture. *Medallion Papers,* No. 25. Gila Pueblo, Globe.

HAURY, E. W.
- 1936a Some Southwestern Pottery Types, Series IV. *Medallion Papers,* No. 19. Gila Pueblo, Globe.
- 1936b The Mogollon Culture of Southwestern New Mexico. *Medallion Papers,* No. 20. Gila Pueblo, Globe.
- 1950 A Sequence of Great Kivas in the Forestdale Valley, Arizona. In *For the Dean,* edited by Erik Reed and Dale King, pp. 29–39. Hohokam Museums Association and Southwestern Monuments Association, Tucson and Santa Fe.
- 1956 Speculations on Prehistoric Settlement Pattern in the Southwest. In "Prehistoric Settlement Patterns in the New World," edited by Gordon Willey, pp. 3–10, *Viking Fund Publications in Anthropology,* No. 23. Wenner-Gren Foundation for Anthropological Research, New York.
- 1957 An Alluvial Site on the San Carlos Indian Reservation, Arizona. *American Antiquity,* Vol. 23, No. 1, pp. 2–27. Salt Lake City.

HAWLEY, F. M.
- 1936 Field Manual of Prehistoric Southwestern Pottery Types. *University of New Mexico Bulletin,* No. 291, *Anthropological Series,* Vol. 1, No. 4. Albuquerque.

HRDLICKA, ALES
- 1952 *Practical Anthropometry,* 4th edition. Edited by T. D. Steward, Wistar Institute of Anatomy and Biology, Philadelphia.

MARTIN, P. S.
- 1943 The SU Site: Excavations at a Mogollon Village, Western New Mexico, Second Season. *Field Museum of Natural History, Anthropological Series,* Vol. 32, No. 2. Chicago.
- 1954 The Mogollon Culture in Western New Mexico. *Southwestern Lore,* Vol. 20, No. 1, pp. 1–4. Boulder.

MARTIN, P. S. AND J. B. RINALDO
- 1940 The SU Site: Excavations at a Mogollon Village, Western New Mexico, 1939. *Field Museum of Natural History, Anthropological Series,* Vol. 32, No. 1. Chicago.
- 1947 The SU Site: Excavations at a Mogollon Village, Western New Mexico, Third Season. *Field Museum of Natural History, Anthropological Series,* Vol. 32, No. 3. Chicago.

1950a Turkey Foot Ridge Site: A Mogollon Village, Pine Lawn Valley, Western New Mexico. *Fieldiana: Anthropology,* Vol. 38, No. 2. Chicago Natural History Museum, Chicago.

1950b Sites of the Reserve Phase, Pine Lawn Valley, Western New Mexico. *Fieldiana: Anthropology,* Vol. 38, No. 3. Chicago Natural History Museum, Chicago.

MARTIN, P. S., J. B. RINALDO, AND E. A. BLUHM

1954 Caves of the Reserve Area. *Fieldiana: Anthropology,* Vol. 42. Chicago Natural History Museum, Chicago.

MARTIN, P. S., J. B. RINALDO, E. A. BLUHM, AND H. C. CUTLER

1956 Higgins Flat Pueblo, Western New Mexico. *Fieldiana: Anthropology,* Vol. 45, Chicago Natural History Museum, Chicago.

MARTIN, P. S., J. B. RINALDO, E. A. BLUHM, H. C. CUTLER, AND ROGER GRANGE, JR.

1952 Mogollon Cultural Continuity and Change: The Stratigraphic Analysis of Tularosa and Cordova Caves. *Fieldiana: Anthropology,* Vol. 40. Chicago Natural History Museum, Chicago.

MEGGERS, B. J. (EDITOR)

1956 Functional and Evolutionary Implications of Community Patterning. In "Seminars in Archaeology: 1955," edited by Robert Wauchope, pp. 129–57. *Memoirs of the Society for American Archaeology,* No. 11. Salt Lake City.

NESBITT, P. H.

1938 Starkweather Ruin. *Logan Museum Publications in Anthropology, Bulletin,* No. 6 Beloit.

OLSON, A. P. AND W. W. WASLEY

1956 An Archaeological Traverse Survey in West-Central New Mexico. In *Pipeline Archaeology,* edited by Fred Wendorf, Nancy Fox, and O. L. Lewis, pp. 256–390. Laboratory of Anthropology and Museum of Northern Arizona, Santa Fe and Flagstaff.

RINALDO, J. B. AND E. A. BLUHM

1956 Late Mogollon Pottery Types of the Reserve Area. *Fieldiana: Anthropology,* Vol. 36, No. 7. Chicago Natural History Museum, Chicago.

SAYLES, E. B.

1945 The San Simon Branch: Excavations at Cave Creek and in the San Simon Valley: Material Culture. *Medallion Papers,* No. 34. Gila Pueblo, Globe.

TUTHILL, CARR

1947 The Tres Alamos Site on the San Pedro River, Southeastern Arizona. *The Amerind Foundation,* No. 4. Dragoon.

WASLEY, W. W.

1957 *The Archaeological Survey of the Arizona State Museum.* Arizona State Museum, University of Arizona, Tucson.

WENDORF, FRED
- 1950 A Report on the Excavation of a Small Ruin near Point of Pines, East Central Arizona. *University of Arizona Bulletin,* Vol. 21, No. 3, *Social Science Bulletin,* No. 19. Tucson.

WHEAT, J. B.
- 1952 Prehistoric Water Sources of the Point of Pines Area. *American Antiquity,* Vol. 17, No. 3, pp. 185–96. Salt Lake City.
- 1954 Crooked Ridge Village (Arizona W:10:15). *University of Arizona Bulletin,* Vol. 25, No. 3, *Social Science Bulletin,* No. 24. Tucson.
- 1955 Mogollon Culture Prior to A.D. 1000. *Memoirs of the Society for American Archaeology,* No. 10. Salt Lake City.

WHEAT, J. B., J. C. GIFFORD, AND W. W. WASLEY
- 1958 Ceramic Variety, Type Cluster and Ceramic System in Southwestern Pottery Analysis. *American Antiquity,* Vol. 24, No. 1, pp. 34–47. Salt Lake City.

WILLEY, G. R.
- 1953 Prehistoric Settlement Patterns in the Virú Valley, Perú. *Bureau of American Ethnology, Bulletin* 155. Smithsonian Institution, Washington.

CONTRIBUTIONS TO POINT OF PINES ARCHAEOLOGY

1. Tree-Ring Dates from Point of Pines. T. L. SMILEY. *Tree-Ring Bulletin,* Vol. 15, No. 3, pp. 20–1. Tucson, 1949.

2. Painted Stone Slabs of Point of Pines, Arizona. C. C. DI PESO. *American Antiquity,* Vol. 16, No. 1, pp. 57–65. Menasha, 1950.

3. A Report on the Excavation of a Small Ruin near Point of Pines, East Central Arizona. FRED WENDORF. *University of Arizona Bulletin,* Vol. 21, No. 3, *Social Science Bulletin,* No. 19. Tucson, 1950.

4. Prehistoric Water Sources of the Point of Pines Area. J. B. WHEAT. *American Antiquity,* Vol. 17, No. 3, pp. 185–96. Salt Lake City, 1952.

5. Four Late Prehistoric Kivas at Point of Pines, Arizona. T. L. SMILEY. *University of Arizona Bulletin,* Vol. 23, No. 3, *Social Science Bulletin,* No. 21. Tucson, 1952.

6. Crooked Ridge Village (Arizona W:10:15). J. B. WHEAT. *University of Arizona Bulletin,* Vol. 25, No. 3, *Social Science Bulletin,* No. 24. Tucson, 1954.

7. Mogollon Culture Prior to A.D. 1000. J. B. WHEAT. *Memoirs of the American Anthropological Association,* No. 82. Menasha, 1955. (Also issued as *Memoirs of the Society for American Archaeology,* No. 10.)

8. "Clean Fill" at Point of Pines, Arizona. L. A. HEINDL. *Kiva,* Vol. 20, No. 4, pp. 1–8. Tucson, 1955.

9. Point of Pines Phase Sequence and Utility Pottery Type Revisions. D. A. BRETERNITZ, J. C. GIFFORD, AND A. P. OLSON. *American Antiquity,* Vol. 22, No. 4, pp. 412–6. Salt Lake City, 1957.

10. An Alluvial Site on the San Carlos Indian Reservation, Arizona. E. W. HAURY. *American Antiquity,* Vol. 23, No. 1, pp. 2–27. Salt Lake City, 1957.

11. A New Type of Ceremonial Killing at Point of Pines. W. J. ROBINSON. *Kiva,* Vol. 23, No. 3, pp. 12–14. Tucson, 1957.

12. Evidence at Point of Pines for a Prehistoric Migration from Northern Arizona. E. W. HAURY. In "Migrations in New World Culture History," edited by R. H. THOMPSON, pp. 1–8. *University of Arizona Bulletin,* Vol. 29, No. 2, *Social Science Bulletin,* No. 27. Tucson, 1958.

13. Excavations at Nantack Village, Point of Pines, Arizona. D. A. BRETERNITZ. *Anthropological Papers of the University of Arizona,* No. 1. Tucson, 1959.